The
Winter
House

and Other Christmas Stories
from Atlantic Canada

NIMBUS
PUBLISHING LTD

Nimbus Publishing Limited
3731 Mackintosh St, Halifax, NS B3K 5A5
(902) 455-4286 nimbus.ca

Printed and bound in Canada
Design: Jenn Embree

FSC
www.fsc.org

MIX

Paper from
responsible sources

FSC® C016245

Library and Archives Canada Cataloguing in Publication

The winter house : and other Christmas stories
from Atlantic Canada.
ISBN 978-1-55109-862-3

1. Christmas—Atlantic Provinces. 2. Christmas stories, Canadian (English)—Atlantic Provinces. 3. Atlantic Provinces—Social life and customs.

GT4987.15.W65 2011   394.266309715   C2011-903898-6

Canada

The Canada Council | Le Conseil des Arts
for the Arts | du Canada

NOVA SCOTIA
Communities, Culture and Heritage

Nimbus Publishing acknowledges the financial support for its publishing activities from the Government of Canada through the Canada Book Fund (CBF) and the Canada Council for the Arts, and from the Province of Nova Scotia through the Department of Communities, Culture and Heritage.

Contents

Christmas Memories

Introduction
Bruce Nunn

In the big white house on that cold December night, the kids were in bed. They listened to the winter wind, and to the air brakes of trucks on the highway just beyond the small woods and on the other side of Kell's farm. A thumping downstairs at the front door made the dog bark. What was it? Their father dressed, went down, and opened the door. There was no one there—just white flurries falling in the darkness. But he saw footprints in the fresh snow. He took a flashlight and went into the swirling night with the family dog, Gomer, sniffing the trail. They followed it down the bank, through the woods, and across Mr. Kell's snowy field. The footprints ended at the highway. There was a man standing by his car. He had been heading home to Sydney, Cape Breton, with a car full of gifts to spend Christmas with his family, but he'd run out of gas. The children's father returned to the house, got some gas they used for the lawnmower, and brought it back to the man, who then continued his yuletide journey home.

It was a short and simple bedtime story, but we liked it. My siblings and I were the kids in bed, hopped up on pre-Christmas jitters. Our father, the storyteller, was working off-the-cuff to get us young 'uns to go to sleep. Our white house with red shutters was in small-town Atlantic Canada. It is one of those towns that, at Christmastime, looks straight out of Dickens: all garlands and lights on snow-covered houses, the gong of the church bell wafting through snowflakes as folks make their way to midnight mass.

But Christmas is a montage of memories, a soft amalgam of nostalgia-wrapped tradition tinged with melancholy, a time when happiness and wistfulness teeter together on a narrow fence.

I see my father's long, thin arm, his white sleeve rolled up, reaching impossibly into the flames of the fireplace as we cheer and clap, to let loose our letters to Santa so they can float up the chimney to the North Pole. Such joy! I see him, too, at the front door in his long coat, let out of the hospital to spend one last Christmas with us.

I see pyjama-ed kids with bed-head, up too early on Christmas morning, and the toys, candy canes, gift wrap, camera flashes, and Christmas stockings, each with an orange stuffed in its toe. I see my mother, bleary eyed, up at 4 AM to put the turkey in the oven—then in later years, on her own with us after Dad's December death. And still each year, the wreath was hung on the red door, the Santa-face cups set out at dinner, the manger scene arranged in the hall—everything decked and draped, and smelling of fruitcakes, cookies, and family-sized meals. Struggle met strength. Loss met love. Christmas carried on.

Several stories in this collection offer a similar theme, wonderful tales of the spirit triumphant in hardship and harshness. Others reflect on hard truths undiminished by the season's celebrations.

The cultural character of our region is captured unveneered in these yuletide tales by some of the best writers these shores have known. Some are full of cheerful poignancy, like Ernest Buckler's "Return Trip to Christmas," and "The Winter House" by Gary L. Saunders. Others are more sombre, like David Adams Richards's observations on the hypocrisies of the season in "The Child and the Boy," or Alden Nowlan's window on Atlantic culture in "Will Ye Let the Mummers In?" Then there's L. M. Montgomery's "A Christmas Mistake," a cherished gem.

These are our stories, and each has its own flavour. You are holding a lovely Pot of Gold mixture of Atlantic Canadian literary treats. I recommend you curl up by the fire and indulge. Go ahead—it's Christmas.

Christmas Stories

The Child and the Boy
David Adams Richards

David Adams Richards wrote "The Child and the Boy"
when he was nineteen years old.

As they walked, they were cold, and would stamp their feet for warmth and walk faster for warmth and wave their arms like wings of wounded birds for warmth. But always they were cold and the clean air of night cut into their bones and they spoke only whispers and never laughed too much.

They would stop as cars passed to throw out their thumbs, hoping. But the cars would pass, leaving only fumes against some air. Then the road would be black and they would move down it, all hope gone.

Everything was black as they walked, their hearts sunken inside and their hair twisted back, statued on their heads from the ice of the air. No moon and only a few cornered stars. The belly of the sky was deep and black. They walked one behind the other, fearing if they spoke too loudly their lungs would freeze like a cup of water or their mouths become caves of ice.

And all along the road, nothing. A whisper or two of snow would scuttle the marking of their boots and now and then a sound behind the trees. But they never noticed sight or sound, for their eyes were down into the collars of their jackets and their hands were rubbed in pockets or twisted under the pits of their arms. Their eyes would at once open and at once clamp shut.

It was the younger one who walked behind, and he was ten. Though he didn't mind the cold so much, now, for he would look up and see his older brother straight ahead always moving. And he would move also and feel satisfied. And he carried the parcels from town and felt that he needed to carry them. He kept his hands warm by shoving them, one at a time, into the thin of his jacket pocket and he would shift the parcel from arm to arm and now and then he would speak.

"Is it already past supper?"

"Yes," his brother would say.

"Far past?"

"Yes," again.

Then silence and cold on their faces, and their ears were numb so they didn't mind them anymore. Then a car and then nothing.

"How many more miles to home?"

"Very many—keep walking."

So Paul kept walking behind his brother and the parcels hurt his arms, but he never told. His older brother was sixteen and healthy and big and looked older than sixteen perhaps. And now that he was sixteen, he had left school to work in the woods. He felt lucky that he had money this Christmas and bought a present for everyone. And he had bought Paul a new coat but hadn't told him yet.

So they moved along the road and the black trees creaked in their frozen roots and the stab of the air bent them more and more. Still there was no drive. And when they passed the drifted houses that were scattered here and there, they heard the inside Christmas music and felt warm for an instant.

But now even the bottoms of their feet were numb and the miles that dragged behind them seemed only to create the miles that stretched before.

"Can we stop and rest?"

"No."

"Why not?"

"Do you want me to carry the presents, now?"

"No."

Paul still went to school. He didn't like it. When he got as old as his brother, he too would quit to work in the woods. Their father would rather see them work. And he didn't like school very much.

The houses that they passed were lighted for the season, and the Santas in the windows laughed emptily through their beards and the dressed trees flinched in the darkness and the topping stars moaned a shallow complaint of light. And as they passed the houses they stared inside for a long moment before pushing drearily along.

"Can we stop and rest?"

"No."

"Why not?"

"We'll freeze if we stop."

"I'm freezing now."

Then they were silent again for a long time, and the older one knew that his brother was cold and much too young to be out like this. He knew his brother was very tiny and would never grow as strong as he.

He had shopped all day and had spent his money, and Paul had trudged wearily beside him, all day. The bus had brought them to town for one dollar each, but they had no money after they ate to take the bus home again. The only drive took them to the far end of town and let them out in the winter cold to walk.

But it was daylight when they had started and now it was very dark and the darkness poured like blood from the wounds of the sky. And every now and then, Paul said he heard animals in the woods and wouldn't want to meet a big animal now. But it was only the wind, his brother told him, and it was silly to be afraid of wind.

Paul was happy when his brother told him he was going to town, and his mother was glad that Paul went, for she didn't need him in the house all day. And he just looked at everything that his little eyes would meet and wondered at the beauty of the lighted town. Now he almost wished he hadn't come.

They were both hungry and could feel their bellies claw at the empty cup of their guts. But they had no food with them so they did without and never spoke of food. And Paul wished he hadn't left half his hamburger on the plate or turned away from his fries. His older brother was right when he said he should eat it all. His brother had paid for it.

"Can we rest now—just for a minute?"

"No."

Then they were silent again for a time, and the older boy thumbed a car that drifted past. Then he turned and faced the younger brother. "There's a house down the road a way and it's the last one for miles and if we don't get a ride we'll stop and ask for help—OK?"

"OK," said Paul and at once a smile cracked the frost of his cheeks and he felt good that his brother was with him.

The house stood alone, a bare house, a poor support for winter. And they neared it slowly, for wind cut into them and drifted through their flesh. Now Paul was tired and the ice had made him raw. But they came upon the house where two lights stabbed their eyes and they stopped and spoke. The road held nothing.

"Will we go in?" asked Paul.

"Yes, we'd better or we'll freeze—I'll talk to them and maybe they'll help us."

"Good," and then he closed his eyes as if to deeply think.

Paul was first to the porch but he let his brother knock, for maybe he hadn't the strength himself to rap, for maybe his hands were now too numb. The older brother knocked. He had broad woodsman's hands and scars that laced his knuckles. No answer. Again he rapped—the pane, a rattle, as if the wind had made the sound. Christmas music softly throated against the empty walls.

Then he rapped a third time and a man edged his face around the curtains. A woman's voice questioned him but they never heard the question, they only gazed at the man who gazed back through the pane. "Yes?" as he opened the door. Paul laid the parcels on the porch and waved his arms. The older boy spoke, almost frightened of his request, almost ashamed to ask for help. This was the first time Paul had heard him speak in so strange a tone.

"We were hiking, sir, and there is no drives and maybe we could come in and get warm for a while?"

"Who's that?" the woman asked beside the man.

"Two Indians want to come in the house."

"Lord no—close the door, are they drunk?"

"I think one is—I smell wine somewhere."

"I'm not drunk, sir," but already the door was jammed shut and the warmth that had crawled about their faces for a minute was gone. They heard the woman speak and then the door lock and they moved into darkness at the foot of the porch.

They stood looking back, silent. Paul walked up the steps again and grabbed his parcels. The older brother rolled a cigarette and urinated in the snow.

"Boys—I'm freezin'," Paul mumbled.

"Maybe we'll build a fire later."

"Good."

Then they walked along the road until they couldn't hear the music anymore.

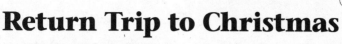

Return Trip to Christmas
Ernest Buckler

*This version of "Return Trip to Christmas" was origi-
nally published in the collection* Thanks for Listening,
edited by Marta Dvorak.

It must have been Friday, because that's the day Mother always cleaned the lamps. I was sitting at the corner of the
kitchen table, cracking walnuts for the Christmas fudge. I
was ten, then. I can see her now—after she'd washed and
dried the chimneys, misting her breath inside them and polish-
ing them until they shone. I had the foolish notion that the shine
came from some delicate vitality in her breath that she could ill
afford to spend. She wasn't a fragile woman, but she looked like
Helen Hayes looks sometimes in a play.

I knew Mother wasn't sick; she never complained, she never
put a hand to any part of her body involuntarily. But sometimes
she would stare at the most familiar object for the longest time. It
wasn't much; merely the sort of thing you avoid doing except in
the presence of children—forgetting that children are the first to
sense it. Father wouldn't have noticed at all.

She got up off her chair when Father came in for a dry pair
of mittens. He was hauling wood. She often sat down at her work
lately and she always sprang up when Father came through the
door. It wasn't in the least that Father was intolerant or unfeeling

about anyone else's weakness. But he was so rock-strong and solid himself—*his* was an almost Scandinavian appearance—that just to look at him made you feel that all listlessness of your own must be fancied or a defect of will. I had something of the same reaction about being inside the house.

"You can finish these now, can't you?" I said to Mother, as if it were only to oblige her that I was cracking walnuts.

I got my mittens off the oven door and went out to the porch for my cap. I couldn't be comfortable in the kitchen while he was in the dooryard unloading. There was nothing I could lift, but I could make a show of loosening the bunks on the chains and, when the sleds were clear again, hook the chains over the back bench and wind their loose ends around the peavey stock.

Father glanced at what Mother was doing. "How would it be if I got you one o' them hangin' lamps for the front room...for Christmas?" he said self-consciously.

Mother was a moment replying. And then she said, "Well, they're real nice, Arth, but now I don't want you to go...."

I knew what made Mother hesitate. Father "thought he was doing something" and it would be too shameful to think about to show disappointment. But a hanging lamp would be the worst gift possible. I knew that her heart was wistfully set on electric lights—however much her head contradicted it and though her tongue never mentioned them. That particular gift would be like the time I had let my imagination play with the picture of these trim hunting boots with red scalloped tops in the catalogue, and he had brought me home the stub rubbers as a surprise. As the hanging lamp would be, they were the best of their kind. So uncompromisingly sturdy and reinforced at all points of greatest wear that it seemed as if I could never escape them.

My mind sputtered to itself. *What do we want of an old hangin' lamp? Why can't we have the lights, like everyone else?* I banged a stick of wood against the side of the woodbox.

Electric lights were a small miracle to us then. No other country place had them. It just happened that the new power line went through our village on its route to the big central dam. Almost everyone else in the neighbourhood got them in by paying so much a month on the installation cost.

That we didn't have them was just an instance of what was typical in Father. I never knew a more generous man, but he'd have nothing whatever that he couldn't pay cash down for. I remember one spring grain was sky-high, he let a whole five-acre ploughed field go unseeded because the storekeeper couldn't even persuade him to accept a month's credit.

"You'd never guess what's goin' on over to Stan Wheeler's this mornin'," he said to Mother.

"No," Mother said. "What?"

"They're puttin' in a radio!" Radios were still a novelty, even in town. "Stan told me himself he only paid twenty-five dollars down on his lights...and...now a radio!" He must be runnin' his face for every *cent* o' that. Where is that man's...?"

Mother shook her head and gave a little laugh of bewilderment. "Don't ask me," she said. "Debt don't seem to mean any more to them than...."

Mother always sided in with him. He wasn't in the least over-bearing. But because he was the sort of man to whom the truth about things seems to be so plainly legible—and because we loved him so much for being the kind of person who'd be utterly helpless to know how to win anyone's love if it weren't given to him natu-rally, and because his love for us was of such bedrock certainty—it never occurred to us he might be mistaken in any of his attitudes. Whenever we were tempted to think differently about anything, it seemed like a failing we should know better than to indulge.

That's why I felt guilty even as I continued my silent sputter-ing. *Yes, yes. We never get anything until we can afford it. After it's an old story to everyone else. It's no fun that way.* I banged another stick of wood against the side of the box.

"Peter!" Mother called. "What in the world are you doing out there in the porch?"

"Nothing," I grunted.

I stood in front of the oxen while Father unloaded the sleds, to give myself the appearance of having a function. Once in awhile I'd shout "Whoah!" though they'd given no sign whatever of starting ahead.

Father never smiled at these transparent little actions of mine. He never treated me like a child when I wanted to be treat-ed like a grownup. On the other hand, he could almost always sense when I wanted to be treated like the child I was, and never, then, treated me like a man.

I watched him toss the leaden beeches into the pile as if they were fence posts, and I forgot about things like lights. He seemed like everything anchored and sustaining. I had never heard him mention anything selfish *he* wanted in my whole life. And one of those sudden little vertigos of exaltation which had spun inside me at odd moments all week possessed me then.

Because this was the enchanted week before Christmas. Snow had fallen steadily until finally the branches of the spruces on the mountain were lipped with pure white, and the frozen wheel ruts in the road were evened over, and everything rough and harsh and plaintive from the fall seemed to be soothed into a dreamless sleep. It was the week when everything had a face. The days...the nights...the kitchen, alive with the intoxicating smell of oranges and spices...the closets, delicious with secret packages. The room where the tree already stood, even though the tree had no trimming yet, really breathed, you could almost see it. And a child, used to being fenced off in the company of his own years, might look into the face of an adult and see, miraculously for a moment, the face of another child.

I looked at Father's face.

He was watching the operation over at Stan Wheeler's. They were putting up the radio aerial. "Well now, if that ain't...." he said to himself. His face was completely encased in incredulity at anything so outlandish.

Then he turned to me. "Do you want to go back with me this trip?" he said.

"No," I said, my voice suddenly short. "I guess I'll stay home and help Mother. I don't think she feels any too good."

"Don't feel good?" Father said. "Who said? Did she say?"

"No," I said. "She'd never let on till she dropped." It was the old-fashioned speech of an only child. "I don't think she's what you'd call sick," I added. "I think...she's just old before she's young."

It was ridiculous talk for anyone my age, and of course I was just mouthing phrases I'd heard my elders use on occasion. And yet I half knew what I was talking about just the same. Mother was forever picturing little refinements that would take the bareness off mere sufficiency, and tracing out her dream of them down to the last detail, even though common sense told her there wasn't the slightest chance of their ever becoming fact. And Father was so....No, "practical" isn't the word, it wasn't anything as cold as that. He never disputed or ridiculed our fancies, they were simply harmless. But for anyone to be always coming up against being made to see that your habit of mind was a vacant one....Until you got so you stared that way at things you held in your hand.

"She just sets and stares at things sometimes," I said.

Father made no comment whatever. "All right," he said. "You stay and help her."

"It ain't her *work*," I started to say, contradicting what I'd said before. But it was quite beyond me to explain what I'd mean by that, so I didn't answer him.

I glanced at Father when the ponderous oxen, with the gait like movement stunned, turned into the bend of the log road beyond the barn. He was hunched forward a little on the sled bench, striking the thumb-and-forefinger angle of one mittened hand inside the same angle of the other. He had that look of the big, forthright man who doesn't quite know what it is that's on his mind, let alone how to work it out. Then, I wished there was something I could side with him against.

At the dinner table that noon he said to Mother all of a sudden, "Annie, why don't you take a little trip down to see Ella before Christmas?" It came out startlingly loud from having been over-rehearsed to sound casual.

Mother was so embarrassed she didn't know where to look.

Ella was her sister in the city. She was married to quite a well-off man quite a bit older than herself and she "had everything." They'd been down to visit us a couple of times. Uncle Clyde's automobile was sleek as a racehorse, with so much room in it that everyone could sit sideways and talk to each other just as if you were in the house. And when he drove us into town, with him and Aunt Ella looking so much more sophisticated dressed *down* than we did dressed up, and when his urbane desk hands (ours were like naïve faces) did their transactions in store after store I directed him to in his search for some special city food that half the storekeepers had never heard of, I kept praying all the time that everyone I knew would see us.

Father didn't have a jealous bone in his body, and you couldn't say exactly that he and Uncle Clyde didn't get along. But when Uncle Clyde would tag along with him at his work and ask him questions about it, as if his interest in this extraordinary way of making a living were some kind of flattery—or when, in all innocence, Aunt Ella would say to Mother, "Oh dear, Annie, I'm so *used* to throwing all our scraps in the garbage, I forget you save them for the pig," or when she'd take the pitcher of hot water in the morning for Uncle Clyde to wash in the spare room basin— Father's face would go kind of set.

I remember one day Uncle Clyde said to him, "Could you make use of these old pants if I left them here when I go back, Arth? In fact, I must have all kinds of castoffs you could get a turn out of, for everyday. Ella could bundle them up and mail them to you."

"They'd be too small for me," Father replied, but the way he looked Uncle Clyde up and down said more than that.

Except for the usual standing invitation, only once before had the question of Mother's going to visit them come up. Aunt Ella had written, asking her to come on a specific date. She'd added a PS: "Clyde says to tell you not to worry about expense. It won't cost you a cent. He'll send you a round ticket."

"By God," Father exclaimed, when Mother read that part out to him, "when I can't pay my own wife's way anywhere...."

Mother folded the letter as if his voice had been a blow on her hands, and when she wrote back to Aunt Ella that night she stared and stared at the pen before she could get the (what possible?) words on the paper. She and Father had never mentioned it again.

That's why she was so taken back now. She didn't know anything about our conversation that morning.

"You know I couldn't go now, Arth," she said. "I'd need clothes, and...."

"Well, *get* clothes," he said.

"And it's such a busy time. No, I couldn't," she added, as if she were stamping firmly on a little flame of yearning that had sprung up in spite of her, "I couldn't."

"You got your cooking all done, ain't you?" he said, "and your presents all wrapped?"

"Yes, but...."

"Well, then...."

"Would you go too?" she said.

It was his turn to look confounded. "Me?" he said. "No. What would I want to go for? I got my wood to get out of this snow, and....But that needn't make no odds to you goin'. It'd give you a change." He hesitated a moment. "You never have any pleasure." Mother looked as if she wanted to cry.

I felt like she did, I didn't know why. I was all confused. I knew that again Father "thought he was doing something," and I knew how hard it must have been for him to come out with this particular suggestion. I knew how totally a gift it was, because he could never understand why anyone should *need* a change.

But again his gesture was subtly wrong. If he'd pitch in with us and said he'd go too, the heck with the wood....But how could Mother go off in a holiday spirit alone, even though it wasn't begrudged to her one iota, even though he urged it on her? Why couldn't people like Father see that no outward "change" whatever which they might arrange for you could take the place of an inward change in *themselves*? And wasn't this week in any way special for him as it was for everyone else, that he wouldn't specially mind being separated from us during it?

Yet I felt the same little flicker of longing as Mother. At Aunt Ella's—where everything that was luxury to us here would be like an everyday thing, without any need for conscience about it. And I had never been to the city. The city, this particular week, with its special excitement....

"Now you just make up your mind to get ready and go," Father said. "I'll drive you to the train tomorrow and come meet you on the train back Christmas Eve. I got to go into town that day anyway."

"What about the tree?" Mother said.

"Trim it that night," Father said. "Or if there ain't time, trim it Christmas Day."

Christmas Day? I thought, in a kind of incredulous horror.

"I couldn't," Mother said again. But now I could see that something fresh was complicating her indecision: a conscience about going against Father's wish, and a weakening before his will. "I couldn't content myself, with you worrying along here all alone."

"Me and Pete can run the ranch here all right, can't we, Pete?" Father said.

"Sure," I said.

It was my automatic agreement with anything Father asked of me. But I'm afraid it came out pretty limp. It had never occurred to me that Father would assume I'd stay here with him. My dream of the city crumpled down over my breath like a kite sailing high in the sky when the wind suddenly fails.

And yet, when I gave it second thought....To be a full partner with Father, just the two of us, in the management of everything on the place. Planning adult things together, and joking together when either of us, as men, were clumsy with some woman's task in the house. *We* could trim the tree, and Mother would be amazed at what a good job we'd do.

I looked at him looking at me as an equal and I felt tall. My heart gave a great surge. Why, this would be *better* than going!

"Now, we both want you to go, why don't you go?" I said to Mother.

The next morning, Father didn't take the oxen to the woods. He said he'd chop a load ahead and come out early to drive Mother to the train.

Mother had decided she'd get Aunt Ella to help her pick out a new dress in the city, and make the rest of her clothes do. "I don't see anything wrong with that hat, do you, Arth?" she said.

"No," he said, "I always thought that was a pretty hat."

I felt curiously hurt for both of them, as if for a moment *they* were the children, to know that it wasn't any kind of hat whatever for the city, but I didn't say anything.

Mother kept posting me: "Now don't forget, the buttermilk pies are in the cellar-way, under the cheesecloth. You better eat them up first, they won't keep like the apple," and, "Remember to keep the cover on the breadbox," and, "You can cook yourself some eggs, they're hearty and they're easy to get." And I kept saying,

"Yes, yes." But I was scarcely listening. I could handle things all right! Again, it was with Father that I felt the team spirit. Men didn't ding at you the way women did.

Around ten o'clock, I thought: *I'll go water the oxen, and he won't have* that *to do when he gets home from the train.* I'd never watered them before, but heightened with my new responsibility I felt equal to anything now.

Father always led them out to the tub one at a time, by the horn. Bright had his head down in the manger, using his long tongue like a hook to lash strands of hay through the chinks in the cow stall next to him. I took hold of one horn to try out the feel of it before I undid his chain. He swung his head up and sideways (I was on the wrong side, to lead him), and I felt the iron strength of his neck go like a charge through my arm. I let go and reached down the whip from the yoke rack behind them. I'd just undo their chains and team them out and back.

Brown made a kind of calf caper and took a playful hook at one of the cows he passed, but it wasn't until they were both out in the yard that I saw what a mistake I'd made to turn them out together. I remembered too late how they always acted the first day Father turned them out to pasture in the spring. How he always screwed the blunt brass knobs onto the points of their horns beforehand.

You wouldn't have believed that these were the same stupefied beasts that had stood side by side in the barn and lumbered along in yoke sluggish as stones, taking no more notice of each other, though their bellies touched, than if they were blind. I watched from the barn doorstep, dismayed.

They acted as if the touch of the ground drove them mad. They raced up and down and criss-cross the yard like runaway horses. They braked their front feet suddenly and arched their backs and threw their rumps up in the air and from side to side like someone snapping a whip. They got down onto their front knees and battled the snowbank with their horns, tossing their heads back and forth like a dog worrying a bone, and when they stood up again, their big eyes rolling in their snow-whitened faces gave them a frenzied look.

"Bright!" I shouted. "Brown! Git over there and drink!" I cracked the whip.

If oxen can sneer, they sneered. Brown did pause for a minute at the tub and push the ice cakes back with his nose to clear a drinking space, and I let out my breath. But he merely tasted the icy water with his teeth and then, disdaining it, tossed his head in the air and started that violent charging again.

And then suddenly they headed for each *other*. I felt the way you do when a grass fire gets out of control like some demon you've unleashed.

Only they weren't running now. They approached each other obliquely, with a deliberation I found more terrifying than anything before. They held their heads down, stalking like cats and seeming to look in another direction, until they were almost touching, and then, *crack!*—I screamed—their horns locked in a flash.

And then there was nothing but that deadly intent buckling against each other with every ounce of their strength. Gaining a foot, losing a foot, breaking free for a few seconds to try to gouge

(I saw a little white pencil mark streak up Bright's side where the hair was laid open and he gave that hollow, unearthly, chilling bark which is the ox's only exclamation), and then, *crack!*, their horns locking again....

I came out of my paralysis and fear. I ran up to them with the whip, striking first one and then the other and screaming, "Bright! Brown! Stop! Stop!" I beseeched them, "Please....Please...." I might have been the wind.

I thought: *the feed boxes.* I raced into the barn and dumped meal into both boxes, banging the boxes against the side of the mangers and shouting, "Come, boy....Come, boy...."

I heard Bright bark again. I ran toward the door with the dipper of meal and just before I got there Bright bounded in, with Brown right behind him. Brown had him on the run. If they keep fighting in the barn, I thought....*If they tackle the cows tied up....What'll I do?*

But each went into his own place as docilely, and buried his nose in the meal box as rapturously, as if nothing had ever happened.

In my crying relief, I crowded between them without the slightest fear, to fasten their chains. I fastened Brown's first. It was shadowy in the mangers and slightly blinding after the sharp sunlight on the snow, and it wasn't until just as I had both arms in position around Bright's bent neck, to drop the bar pin on one end of his chain into the big round link on the other, that I noticed anything wrong. I let the pin fall through as if I were losing my grip on an intolerably heavy stone. Your heart *can* sink. I felt mine do it then.

For where Bright's big, hard left horn should be there was only the "peth" of it now, glistening and streaked with blood like the inside of a rabbit's pelt. That last bark—Brown had knocked its shell right off.

Bright was ruined. You could never strap a yoke on him now. I knew the peth would harden in time, but I knew that Father would never have a stunted, unsightly thing like that in his barn. That's why he'd *bought* this team, because their horn spreads had matched so perfectly.

Father. What would he ever say? But that was the worst part of it. He wouldn't rage at me (if he only would!) or whip me. He'd just....I could see his uncomprehending face.

I stood there, hating myself. The very first thing I'd tried to do....

I stood there and everything was in ruins. Our partnership, Mother's trip, Christmas, everything....You can truly wish that the earth would swallow you up. I stood there and wished desperately that I could turn into nothing.

Such wishes are always denied, of course. And sooner or later you have to make a move of some kind. I went out into the yard. Sure enough, there was the horn. I picked it up. It was still warm.

And then I had this crazy idea. I had knocked down Mother's best platter one time and broken it in two, fishing for the cookie jar. I had stood it up again and fitted the edges together so well that Mother had never known the difference until the next time she came to use it. It wasn't an act of slyness, really; it was just until I could get over that terrible "gone" feeling at the time.

If I could slip the horn back on. I took it back into the barn and I gave Bright another dipper of meal to keep him quiet and my hands were trembling, but I must have got just the right twist on it, for it slipped into place like a glove. Bright paid no more attention to what I was doing than he would to a fly bite.

The horn felt absolutely solid unless you tugged on it. Would there be such a thing that it'd grow back on as good as ever? I should tell Father about it, ask him that. Maybe there was something he should do—tar around the base, to seal it off from the air, I now seemed to remember having heard someone say.

But I just couldn't tell him. I knew it was cowardice, but I knew what I was going to do. I was going away with Mother before he found out. Let him think Bright had loosened his horn somehow in the manger.

I wasn't afraid he'd yoke them up without noticing it. The bleeding had matted a little circle of hair right where the horn joined the head. He'd see that first thing when he went to water them after coming back from the train, and do anything that needed to be done.

The next hour or so I don't even like to remember. White and shaky inside, and sick with the traitorous feeling of secrecy. My heart lurching like a leaf at the clout of a raindrop when I saw Father coming out the log road. Holding my breath while he harnessed the horse—though the horse stable was on this side of the barn, with a separate door—lest something would put it into his head to have a look at the cattle.

I like least of all to remember Father's face when Mother told him I'd "put up a touse" to go with her at the last minute. "Well, if he'd rather," was all he said. I sat speechless on his lap in the sleigh, thinking every minute of the way to town that if he tumbled to my deception before I could make up my mind to confess, he'd never have any faith in me again.

Trips that begin disastrously often rally and become all the more splendid. This one didn't.

Uncle Clyde wasn't there to meet us when we got off the train, though Mother had spent a whole dollar to phone Aunt Ella when we would arrive. We waited almost an hour, hungry, and islanded with strangeness in the gaunt, dusk-dreary station before they appeared. (I told Mother I wasn't hungry at all, because I couldn't bear to think of elbowing our way to those high stools before the counter with the mirror behind it that would keep giving us back our unease, and where the hectic waitresses seemed to slap the food around as if it were something contaminous.) And when they did show up, they exchanged a few peevish words before they greeted us properly.

"I *told* you to call the station and check on the time," Uncle Clyde said. "You might know you wouldn't remember it right."

"Now, just because Tom Carlton gets a raise at Christmas and you don't, don't take it out on me," Aunt Ella said.

Both of them were as nice as could be to *us*, but by turns. It wasn't until we reached the apartment that they joined forces in welcome. The drive there wasn't anything like I'd pictured it would be.

I knew it wasn't because they were in any way ashamed of us, but almost the first thing Aunt Ella said to Mother in the car was, "Annie you ought to wear a hat that's off your face more. Here, try on this one of mine, just for fun. You can have it if it fits you." And I couldn't help noticing Uncle Clyde's eyes smile at my clumsy mail-order cap a whole size too large.

Strangely enough, I didn't much care, though. Uncle Clyde didn't seem like anyone so special *here*. Not the way Father seemed special amongst the men home. Nor did his car, either. In fact, nothing seemed special here. There was so many just like it or a little better.

I felt funny going up in an elevator for the first time. But I felt funnier still that Uncle Clyde and Aunt Ella merely nodded to the neighbours who got off on the same floor, and made no move whatever to "make us known" to them. What would people think if you acted like that with company home?

The apartment was so much finer furnished than any house I'd ever seen as to seem altogether elegant to me. It was like a rich plush pocket you stepped into out of the teeming day. But it was like a pocket in other ways too. Once you'd become familiar with what was strange about it, you couldn't seem to take a dozen steps without meeting yourself coming back. The radio I'd looked ahead to so eagerly was broken. Uncle Clyde explained that he was getting Aunt Ella a new, much bigger, one for Christmas, but she didn't seem to be in the least excited about it. Their Christmas tree was already decorated, and as elegantly as everything else, but it looked like a homesick child you are trying to distract with blandishments.

The whole city struck me like that. Aunt Ella took us to see all the Christmas displays in the big stores, but there seemed to be something iron-grey striking through the glitter of everyone's and everything's faces, like when the stove polish burned off. And all the snow looked soiled.

One night Uncle Clyde said to Mother jokingly, "I suppose kids are easier to satisfy once they know there isn't any Santa Claus. Or is it the other way around?" I had believed in Santa Claus until that moment. And there was nowhere in an apartment where you could go, to be alone for awhile with such a discovery.

That was the night I had the nightmare. On the bed they had to assemble and take apart for me each day. Santa Claus was coming toward me, and just when he got touching close, two ox horns came out of the side of his head and one of them was bleeding.

It was the longest and the shortest week I ever spent. Long and wasteful by the hour, for having had my dream of the city turn out to be such a subtle fraud; and short and chilling by the day for having each one bring me nearer to the showdown with my crippling secret when we got home again.

It wouldn't be anything like the truth to say to Aunt Ella and Uncle Clyde were glad to see us leave. There was an extra spurt of sincere feeling when we said goodbye. But if we'd missed the train or anything, and had to re-open our visit, no one would have been able to conceal the awkwardness of it.

I had little spells of shivering on the train. But it wasn't the usual delicious shivering on the day before Christmas. *This whole lost "week before Christmas,"* I thought...that could have been so different if I'd never set foot inside the barn that morning.

Mother was very quiet too. She wasn't returning to something she dreaded, like I was; but I knew that her "change" hadn't done her any good either. It wasn't one of those changes that makes you fancy the things you are coming back to must have been rejuvenated by it as well, that you'll find them altered in all the ways you've always hoped for. That little rigidity of Father's in certain things would be just the same.

I thought of saying I was sick when the train blew inexorably for our station. For I knew now that Father would be in possession of the whole truth. Think of any plausible deception long enough and some shark's fin is sure to break through its surface. It had come to me not ten minutes ago about the telltale hoof marks in the snow....

I got the surprise of my life.

Father was there to meet us—no fear of *him* getting the time wrong—but however I had expected him to act, this wasn't it. For one thing, he was all shaved and dressed up. And though I couldn't put my finger on exactly what the change in him was, he almost behaved as if *he* were the one that some penitence had taken the starch out of and made awkwardly thoughtful. He had hot bricks for our feet, and....Mother laughed: "Arth, what in the world made you think we'd need the buffalo robe on a mild day like this?" He kept asking us question after question about our trip. He even enquired about Uncle Clyde.

Mother scarcely heeded his questions for plying him with her own about how he had managed by himself.

"It's a shame you had to break up your whole afternoon coming in here to pick us up," she said as we drove out of town. "Just when the hauling was at its best."

"Oh, the wood'll keep," Father said. "There'll be wood after we're dead and gone."

I had never heard Father make a remark like that in my whole life. It too came out awkwardly, but I could tell it wasn't any attitude he was putting on. What had come over him? It was already dark, and I didn't see Mother stare at his face, but I fancied I could feel her doing it. I imagined that a tension went out of the way she was holding herself in the sleigh, as in a limb released from the cramp of one steady position.

But I couldn't exult. I was too consumed with the exasperation you feel when someone, however innocently, goes straight to the very topic you've been dreading.

"And I suppose you could only make two turns a day, with everything else to look after," Mother said. I seemed to shrink up, and my exasperation turned to anger. Oh, *why* couldn't women ever let anything drop! I held my breath for Father's answer. This was the moment.

"Matter o' fact," he said, "I've knocked off haulin' for awhile." He leaned forward and flicked the horse's flank with the tip of the whip. "I got rid o' the oxen."

"Got rid of the oxen?" Mother echoed him. She might have been saying, "Got rid of the place!"

"I'm sleepy," I put in suddenly. It was a dead giveaway, but I couldn't help it. "Can I get down in the front of the sleigh?"

"All right," Father said gently. "Get right down on the bottom and rest your back against my legs."

"Yeh," he said to Mother. "They was gettin' along. And I got a good trade on 'em. Beef's sky high, y'know. The meat man give me a pair o' yearlin' steers and two hundred dollars boot. I had use for the boot."

My whole body breathed out. It was like waking from a nightmare. He was going to let it slide. He wasn't going to mention a thing. Oh, Father....

"I suppose you needed the boot, that's why you sold them," Mother said. "And us wasting your money on this trip!"

"Now, now," Father said. "I guess we ain't gone starve jist yet awhile." I had never heard him make a remark like that before, either.

"But they wasn't old cattle, Arth?" Mother kept at it. "They couldn'ta been more'n seven or eight, were they?"

"Well, no, they wasn't *dead* old," Father said. "But Bright was always either crowdin' or haulin' off. Pete and I kin break these new steers in ourselves, so they'll work right." He added, as if it were the most trivial afterthought, "And Bright'd knocked a horn loose somehow."

"Knocked a horn loose?" Mother exclaimed. "How did he do that? Did you see him when he did it?"

Oh, *Mother*! It was the way she'd kept quizzing me about the platter even after I'd confessed. There hadn't been a suggestion of punishment about it, but why did women have to keep dinging at a thing? When Father....When men....

"Are you comfortable there, Pete?" Father said to me. I didn't answer.

"I guess he's asleep already," Mother said.

"It looks like," Father said. But somehow I was sure he knew better.

"Arth?" Mother harked back. "Didn't you see the ox when he did it? He couldn't do it in the barn, could he?"

"I don't know, I suppose he could," Father said.

"Well, I don't see how," Mother said. "Arth," she continued after a minute, in an entirely different voice, "Peter was up to the barn a long while that morning. You don't suppose that little monkey turned them out or anything...?"

"He might have," Father said. He moved his legs—to rouse me, I think, if I should be really asleep. He must have known by the way I readjusted my body against them that I did it conscious-ly. "But why would he be scared to own up to me about it?" he said slowly. "Surely he don't think I'm that kind of a...."

I turned my cheek flat against his knee and I clasped his leg with my hand for just a moment. He put one hand on my cheek for just a moment. I knew that that was all the exchange that would ever be necessary between us.

I fell asleep that way.

I slept until we were almost home. When I awoke, Mother was still asking him questions. There was a curious—well, kind of freedom—in her voice. I don't know why, but it reminded me of the way a calf that's always been tied up acts when you first let him loose. First he only goes as far as his rope used to let him. Then he ventures a little farther, and stops short, surprised. Then a little farther still, but still doubting. Then a little farther still. Until finally, in one great bound, he *believes* that all limits are gone.

"What did you do with yourself evenings?" she was saying.

"Oh, I don't know," he said. "Stan made me go over and listen to the radio one night, and...."

"That was nice," she said. "How does the radio work?"

"Fine," he said. "Perfect."

"What was on?" she said.

"That night, they was actin' out kind of a play," he said. "*Ile*, they called it."

"I'll?" Mother said. "I'll what?"

"No," he said. "Like kerosene. Oil." I thought about the hanging lamp. "This old whaler captain in the story called it 'ile.' He...." But he stopped short. "I don't know how they kin make them things sound so real," he said.

"Was it really just like real people?" I exclaimed.

"Well!" Father said. "Did you have a good sleep? Yessir, it was just as plain as if you was right there."

It was pitch dark when we drove in the yard, but still early evening. We'd have lots of time to trim the tree. I leapt out of the sleigh. I felt suddenly sorry for Uncle Clyde and Aunt Ella—for everyone in the world who wasn't us. Mother seemed wonderful all over again. *She* didn't know...and what a blessing she *had* kept at the thing until it was all cleared up!

"I'll fetch the lantrun," I said eagerly.

"Just a minute," Father said. "You get the things out the back, till I find the key. Now which pocket...." It was odd that he'd locked the house. We never thought of locking our doors. He was knotting the reins around a big twitch on the woodpile and throwing the rug over the horse. "Wait a minute, now," he said, "till I go ahead and show you where the path is I shovelled out." It was a path to the front door.

We followed him up the path and through the front door. "Are ya in?" he said. "Now don't stumble there, till I get a light."

He went over to the side of the room where the lamp stand was. But he didn't strike a match. He bent down on one knee to the floorboard. And then....

"Merry Christmas," he said. There was an almost sheepish smile on his face.

The sudden light made us blink after the pitch darkness outside. But it wasn't harsh or blinding. It was the soft magic light of I couldn't count how many little coloured bulbs strung over the Christmas tree.

"Arth!" Mother gasped. "Oh, Arth!"

"You never noticed the wires or a thing," he said, "did you? I was afraid you'd notice the pole by the gate."

"Not a single solitary thing!" Mother said, like someone dazed. And then she began to cry.

I couldn't open my mouth. I just ran across the room and hugged him around the waist. I didn't care whether it was childish or not.

Mother fought for control of her voice. "Arth," she said, "they're...it's...I can't tell you. But...."

"But what?" he said.

"But it must have taken every cent you got out of the oxen. I hate to think of you...."

"What's the odds?" Father said. "We're only goin' this way once."

I could hardly believe my ears. And I knew it wasn't the lights then that gave Mother's face that shining look.

"Maybe you won't like the fixtcher I picked out for the kitchen, I don't know," Father said quickly. We followed him into the kitchen with a kind of rapt and speechless obedience. The radio was in the kitchen.

"Turn that knob on the left there," he said to me.

I turned the knob without a word, though I could tell by his eyes that my own must have been glistening. The most exquisite choir I had ever heard came right into the room. "Sing in exultation..."

"I thought first I'd get you one o' them washin' machines," Father said to Mother, "to save you work...and then, I didn't know, I thought maybe you'd just as leave have the radio...."

And that was the finest thing of all. It meant he understood. He really understood at last. We stood there, listening, and three people were never more like one. I knew there wasn't any Santa Claus—but I knew now that there'd always be Christmas.

It wasn't until years later that I found out about *Ile*. That it was the famous play about a hard, inflexible man so proud and set on his own goals that his wife lost her reason from having her womanly fancies so stonily disregarded. That his wife's name was Annie. It gave me the sharpest pang. To think that Father could have imagined for one minute—and maybe because of what I'd said that morning at the woodpile—that there was any likeness whatever of that man in himself.

But I was sure he must have known—certainly from that Christmas on—that *we'd* never thought so.

Lucky Stars
Bob Kroll

Alice Stewart had gone all day without a fire on the hearth. She was cold to the bone. No matter how deep she hunched into her husband's tattered overcoat, no matter how tightly she pulled the patchwork blanket over her head and shoulders and gathered it at her chin, she shook and chattered, and her hands were numb. Perhaps too numb to strike steel and flint. Alice worried. She wiggled her fingers and then, without lowering the blanket from her chin, folded her hands into the coarse woollen cloth.

"One chance," Alice said aloud to the shadows that lengthened over the floorboards. "I have only one chance."

Her words were short and brittle and ready to break under the strain of waiting, waiting, standing at the window and waiting for the sun to set.

Alice was twenty-one, more than two years in clover, and now three months with child. She was a Scottish girl who had met Alexander Stewart on board the transport ship to Nova Scotia. That was two years ago this past September, in 1799, on the Feast of Saint Michael the Archangel. They had fallen in love at sea, then posted bans for marriage within a month of dropping anchor at Pictou Harbour. They had married in November. A small ceremony. A quiet frolic. Then a long walk from New Glasgow to their new log home on the road to Mount Thom.

From their first days together, they shared a common hope and heads full of dreams. If their first year of marriage had been a promise of what was to come, their lives together would have been all sunshine and blue sky. But fine weather can so easily change to grey cloud and drizzle, and for that, Alice blamed herself. Their luck had changed last Christmas Eve, all because she had thoughtlessly extinguished the yule candle with her breath.

"It wasn't your fault," Alexander Stewart had comforted his young wife. Alexander was a straight-backed, hard-working lowland Scot, and he did not believe in superstition. He insisted that his arm getting crushed in the carriage shop last winter was an accident and not a stroke of bad luck. It had nothing to do with Alice blowing out the yule candle on Christmas Eve instead of carefully pressing the flame between her fingers.

But Alice Stewart believed in Christmas superstition. She believed that with a single breath last Christmas Eve, she had blown bad luck into their lives. From the very instant the flame had gone out, Alice had felt a shadow close over her. And from that moment on, she blamed herself for their empty pockets and hungry bellies, and for her husband's droop and sadness because there was so little work for a man who had only one arm.

As Alice looked from the window at the sun edging closer to the earth, the memory of last Christmas Eve shivered in her thoughts. "One chance," Alice repeated to her dim reflection in the glass. "I have one chance to wish our pennies into silver and our silver into gold."

The air was cold and damp. Tree branches dripped blue crystals. In the valley below, slanted roofs seemed diamond-like in the closing light of the setting sun.

Alice felt for the flint and steel in her pocket and looked at the dry kindling on the grate. Everything was ready. All day she had been fussing, following an old neighbour's advice. Soon after her husband had started for New Glasgow to look for a day's work, Alice had doused yesterday's coals and scrubbed the hearth clean of the past year's ashes.

Alice had curried each word for its meaning, and nodded to show the old woman she understood. Then the old woman had leaned close and whispered a warning: "One chance, Alice. You have only one chance. All must be done in that single moment between the glow of sunset and glimmer of starshine. Hesitate, and the chance is lost."

"Cool the coals of misery," the old neighbour had told her, "and sweep away the cinders of regret. Use dry kindling for fire, new wood for smoke. Burn last year's sorrow in the dying light of the sun. And pin this year's promise on the twinkle of the first evening star."

Alice opened the door to the cabin so she could see the sunset from the hearth. She removed the flint and steel from her pocket and knelt before the kindling on the grate.

The sun had lowered, and gleamed rosy on the horizon with the last light of day. Alice struck steel and flint. Clumsily at first, but as her numb hands warmed from the effort, her stokes became harder, faster. Spark after spark danced about her hand, flashing and whirling. One leaped among the tinder. And Alice's heart leaped with it. The spark flared in the kindling, then slowly smouldered and died.

Alice fumbled with the flint and steel. Her heart quickened. She looked out the open door to the blue sky deepening into the painful colours of a bruise. Her back tingled with sweat and the cabin suddenly seemed close and clingy. The patchwork blanket fell from her shoulders onto the floor. The old woman's warning nibbled at the edges of Alice's hope. "All in a single moment. Hesitate, and the chance is lost."

Alice wondered if the moment had passed. She ran from the cabin, swept her eyes over the sky, and saw a single glimmer of starlight. Quickly she turned to the horizon. It still burned with the last light of day. Strangely, the sun seemed to linger like a friend at the door unwilling to say goodnight.

Alice hurried to the hearth. She struck steel against stone again and again, and the flash dancers sparked about her hand and fell among the tinder. There was a sudden flare and a gasp of smoke. Alice nuzzled close to the grate and whispered the smoulder into flame.

She felt the heat on her cheeks and the fire in her eyes. Her spirit brightened and her mouth rose into a smile as she looked through the door at the sliver of sunlight yet hanging on the horizon. Then she wished. With all her might, and on the flames of the yule fire, she wished for good luck and happiness, and raced from the cabin to pin that wish on the twinkle of the first evening star.

But as she spread her arms, threw back her head, and looked into the sky, her mouth fell open and her face ran the colour of winter birch. Instead of one star, there were many. The moment had passed, or so Alice thought. Time had buried the day

All of a sudden the evening became dark, dark, dark. Everything merged: fields, road, sky. And Alice's spirit darkened with it. Lifting heavy feet in clumsy shoes, the young wife trudged into the cabin to find little comfort in the small fire burning on the grate.

It was then she heard her husband's voice singing her name as he climbed the rounding trail to their cabin on the hill. Alexander carried a large leather pouch with the King's Broad Arrow inscribed on the flap. He smiled proudly as he entered the cabin, slipped the pouch from his shoulder, and tossed it onto the deal table. He curled his wife into his arm, swung her off her feet, and kissed her.

"Merry Christmas," he said, and pointed at the pouch. His eyes beamed. He sprinkled his words with laughter. "I went all day without an offer. Walked home in misery. Then, just this moment, Mr. McRae stopped me at the gate. He rode from the town to catch me. Leaned down from his horse and said he had a job for a man with two strong legs. I puffed my chest and answered that I would walk to hell and back. McRae said Halifax was far enough, and reached me the pouch. The mail pouch, Alice. A shilling a month. I'm a courier!"

His words seemed to move like music, playfully reaching into the stillness of her thoughts and dancing with her heart. It was like a wish come true, Alice thought, and that thought bubbled into laughter and had her leading her husband in a jig around the table, out the door, and into the frosty night.

There, she raised her eyes to the scatter of stars across the sky. She had no idea how that single star had circled her wish with starlight, but she believed with a superstitious wonderment that truly it had. And because she did not know which star was her lucky star, Alice simply raised her arms and thanked them all.

The Last Bell
Michael O. Nowlan

Millbank was a quiet little village after the war. The mill had long ceased operation, so most of the men had to look elsewhere for work. It is true there were many pulp and pit-prop boats during the summer, but the work was seasonal. Lumber exports from the region were heavy at the turn of the '50s. It was then that they built the new wharf. Often there would be a ship at each wharf and a couple anchored in the stream waiting to take on cargo.

These ocean-going freighters were the talk of the village. Sailors frequently sold cigarettes and liquor to the workers at well below local prices.

That December morning, however, there were no ships. The famous Miramichi was frozen solid from bank to bank. As the Christmas Eve sun came up over Middle Island, the hustle and bustle of last-minute Christmas preparations filled Millbank households.

The men who had been working at the lumber camps were home for the holiday. Those who worked for the government were also taking Christmas Eve with their families. Trees were dragged out of woodsheds and garages. Some were even cut from nearby woodlots.

In the early morning chill, Jean Luke was giving final instructions to her husband, Albert, as he made a new stand for the tree. As she shivered in the frost, she looked across the barren fields to All Saint's Church. "It's too bad about the bell! I was sure they'd fix it up for Christmas this year."

Albert grunted. "Yeah! I told 'em I'd fix it. But nobody believes ol' Albert."

Albert and Jean lived near the end of the village in a small but comfortable wood hut. Albert bore the brunt of the men's jokes at the general store. He was a hard worker, but few gave him any credit. Two Luke sons had been killed in action during the war. The third now lived in Northern Ontario. There were no girls.

After the tree was settled in the corner of the living room, Albert went up the road to the store. He needed another fig of chewing tobacco. He figured Jean would get him some, but he was not going to count on it. Maybe she would get him something else for Christmas, and he needed his Napoleon to tide him through Christmas.

It was past ten o'clock when he kicked the snow from his boots, pushed the door open, and entered the store. The smell of apples, oranges, and chocolate brought a tingling sensation to his nostrils. It was a smell the store had only at Christmastime. It was your usual country general store. There was not enough room for everything. Goods of all kinds were stacked from floor to ceiling.

The store was one of a chain operated by a well-to-do businessman who now made his home in Halifax. Lloyd Snow, who had managed the Millbank business for many years, was measuring out five pounds of white sugar for John Scott. Both men said "Merry Christmas" as Albert stomped the last of the snow from his boots.

"That time of year again," said Albert in his deep, rasping voice. "Merry Christmas!"

At the back of the store, Joe Smith and his brother Leonard were sitting in front of the checkerboard, which was conveniently arranged on an upturned nail keg. Even though the store was crowded, there was always room for the checkerboard. Tim Hughes stood near the Smith brothers. After they exchanged greetings with Albert, Tim Hughes laughed and said: "Santa Claus comin' to yer old lady, Albert?"

The others laughed.

"He'll come," Albert assured them.

Albert picked up a box of soda biscuits and looked at the large block of cheese in the glass showcase in the corner. *Some cheese and soda biscuits will be a good treat,* he thought. The Lukes didn't have much money. Just what Albert earned from the boats in the summer and snaring a few rabbits in winter. He also cut some pulp for Joe McNeil, but everyone knew Joe didn't pay very good wages.

As he was about to ask Lloyd for a piece of cheese, he overheard Joe Smith: "Nobody around here can fix that bell. I told Father Mooney that last summer and the summer before. There just ain't no sense in harpin' on it like that." He addressed this comment to his brother Leonard. Leonard always thought that since his brother was an expert carpenter, he should have volunteered to do the job.

The bell in All Saint's Church hadn't rung since lightning hit the steeple two and a half years before. Joe and his crew repaired the steeple, but maintained the bell could no longer function because the crossbeam was damaged. It could be repaired only with special timber from British Columbia. Since Joe was the expert, everyone tended to believe him.

Albert looked up and stared at Joe.

"What're you starin' at, you dummy? I said the bell can't be fixed, and that's that."

Albert continued to stare as Tim Hughes laughed. "He told me he could fix it. Imagine that! Albert Luke fixin' the church bell."

Everyone laughed as Lloyd and John joined the others near the nail keg.

By now Albert was angry. He liked these men, but when they treated him like a simpleton, sparks danced in his little dark eyes.

In trembling voice, he said, "Mister Lloyd, I want a piece of that cheese. 'Bout a half-pound."

"Half a pound," snorted Joe. "That won't even feed the mice in your shack."

Again the group laughed loudly.

With his cheese, soda biscuits, and extra fig of Napoleon, Albert turned to leave. He hesitated and looked back at Joe. He shook his finger, and shouted, "I'll fix the bell for midnight Mass."

As the door closed behind Albert, the peals of laughter echoed through the walls of the small frame building.

"I'll show 'em!" Albert muttered as he started down the road.

After lunch, Albert told Jean of his plan to go to the church to fix the bell so "it will ring for the baby Jesus."

Jean was ready to argue, but she knew when Albert had made up his mind. She also knew something must have happened at the store, because Albert was very quiet and appeared upset when he came home.

"You decorate the tree and make supper. I'll have the bell ready by then."

Albert got pieces of two-by-four and some haywire from the shed. He knew if he could raise the old beam to its original level, he should be able to strap it with two-by-fours and haywire. That way it would be almost as good as new. He went to the shelf in the far corner to get an old jack he had picked up in the dump that fall when he was hunting. He knew it would work, for he had tried it under the edge of the shed. Today it had to do the big job. He got saw, axe, hammer, draw bar, and nails. Putting them all on his small hand sled, he trudged off to church.

As he neared the church, he remembered what Jean had said. "Don't fall," were her last words to him as he left the house. He was a little afraid of climbing such heights, but he wanted to show Joe Smith and all the others. The thought occurred to him that he could fall.

While all Millbank got ready to celebrate, Albert spent the afternoon in the church steeple. It was a beautiful winter afternoon. The ice was good enough for crossing, so those who needed last-minute gifts had a short walk to town.

Each family had its Christmas specialty. For the Muldoons, it was homemade doughnuts; the Dickensons had mocha cakes; the O'Tooles had a special cheesecake made with pie crust, cake batter, and cheddar cheese topping; the Smiths used a special fruitcake recipe brought from England by their great-grandmother. And so on. The list was endless.

Each home, of course, had turkey, chicken, or goose, but all Jean Luke had was a roast of beef. She didn't mind, however, for she would roast it just the way Albert liked it. And she would make a smooth brown gravy with lots of onions and carrots in it. There was also a small fruitcake she'd managed to buy with the money Albert Jr. sent from Ontario. Yes. It would be a fine Christmas—except there would be no bell for midnight Mass.

This thought reminded her of Albert. "Where is that man?" she wondered out loud. It was past five and getting dark. "Hope he don't fall!"

At five thirty, she heard him on the stoop as he kicked the snow from his boots and came in from the frosty air. Jean was relieved to see him, but she knew by the look on his face that he did not get the bell to ring.

"I'll get the lantern and go back after I eat," he said.

Oh no, Jean thought. *He can't go back there after dark. He'll be fallin' for sure.* She was convinced the whole idea was senseless.

Again, she only mildly protested as Albert went out into the star-filled Christmas Eve. The lights from the town across the river flooded the sky, and Albert thought he could hear the strains of

"Adeste Fideles" in the air. Maybe he imagined it. Maybe someone had a radio turned up very loud.

Walking back to the church, he thought of another radio. The one he'd bought for Jean. Wouldn't she be surprised! He got it with money from the last boat he worked. He had checked in at lunchtime. It was still safe in the box under the shelf in the shed. Albert Luke was happy. He began to whistle an old Christmas tune his mother taught him.

Just before Lloyd Snow closed the store at eight o'clock (it usually closed at ten, but this was Christmas Eve), Joe Smith stuck his head in the door and yelled to Lloyd, "Old Albert is down there tryin' to fix the bell. Got a lantern an' all. I just seen him. Was there all afternoon too."

Lloyd shook his head. "Hope he don't fall. Make an awful mess an' this bein' Christmas Eve."

"Crazy nut!" Joe said, and he went off into the night.

When Albert didn't return by ten thirty, Jean Luke got worried. "I better get over there." She was talking out loud to herself again.

She knew the carols would start at eleven thirty and she didn't want to miss them. *I'll send him right home to change his clothes*, she thought. She knew Mass would be late starting, for Father Mooney would have many confessions.

"He'll have lotsa time." Once more she spoke out loud.

Jean was the first to arrive at church. It was warm inside, so she knew the furnace was working. Peering up the steeple in to the dim lantern light, she called to Albert.

"You git home an' change. I told you you'd never fix that bell."

"Just a little more an' she'll work," came the rasping voice from high above her. She knew the tobacco juice was thick in his mouth.

For the third time that day, Jean Luke didn't argue. She quietly went into their regular seat and knelt down. "Please, don't let him fall," she whispered.

Votive lights danced reflections about the walls and around the crib. The stillness was broken only by a sudden thud of axe or hammer in the steeple.

Soon the choir members were arriving and Father Mooney was there laying out the vestments. Several people were lining up for confession.

Father Mooney went to the entry of the church and looked up the steeple to the bell platform. "What are you doing, Albert?"

"I'm fixing the bell, Father. She will ring tonight."

Father Mooney attempted to encourage Albert. "That's good. Don't fall." And off he went to hear confessions.

When Joe Smith arrived at 11:55, he was in great humour. "What ye doin' up there Albert? Waitin' for Santa Claus? Them reindeer don't land on church steeples." And his deep-throated laugh echoed throughout the church.

When Jim Norris's horse and sleigh came into the churchyard, the jangle of bells filled the night. The Norrises were the only ones who didn't walk or come by car.

At 12:05, Father Mooney was still in the confessional. The choir singing had stopped and the younger members were fidgety.

Joe Smith and a couple other men stood in the entry, waiting until the Father came into the sanctuary before they would dodge into a back pew.

At 12:08, the ladder shook above the three men, and Albert Luke came down from the bell platform.

"Time ya gave up, ya dummy," Joe said, in a low whisper this time.

Albert stared at him. "I fixed that bell, Joe Smith. Go ahead an' pull that rope. She'll ring now. Go ahead! Pull the rope."

For the first time in his life, Joe Smith was speechless. A limp hand moved toward the rope above his head. Gingerly, he pulled. A faint tinkle of the All Saint's Church bell was heard. Then it became louder. Father Mooney, who was vesting for Mass, missed his prayer and put the wrong knot in his cincture. Joe Smith's wife was so startled, she stood up in her seat. Jean Luke wiped a tear from her cheek.

Albert, still standing by the entry door, said, "I told you, Joe Smith, I'd fix that bell." And he went out to his hand sled with his tools and lantern.

The night was fully Christmas. The moon's reflection cast a silver sheen across the fields, contrasting with the stubble that still poked through in places. The bell echoed the joyous mood of the season.

And the bell pealed out in the Christmas night. Being ten minutes late, it was the last Christmas bell to float its sound over the Miramichi. But to the people of Millbank, there was no bell like it.

As the choir sang "Gloria in excelsis Deo..." Albert Luke slid into the pew beside his wife. Without losing a note in the great hymn of praise, she squeezed his dirty, calloused hand.

Will Ye Let the Mummers In?
Alden Nowlan

Clayton Murdoch, owner of the old Peabody place, awoke, stretched, and felt that life was good. Then he got out of bed, pulled on wool socks, and went to the window, flexing his arm muscles like a boxer. His world, this morning of the twenty-fourth of December, was a monochrome in bluish white. "What time is it?" Barbara said.

With her auburn hair spilling over the shoulders of her long-sleeved nightdress, she looked quite the proper mistress for this 150-year-old house. "I didn't mean to wake you," he said. "It's five to eight." He looked out the window again. Bluish-white fields, bluish-white fences, bluish-white trees, and in the distance two bluish white houses under a bluish-white sky. "The silence," he said, inhaling the wonder of it.

"I don't notice it as much as I did in the summer," Barbara said. "The birds made just enough noise to remind you that noise existed. I miss the birds." From the henhouse, as if on cue, there came the muffled crowing of the rooster they had named Frank Harris. "Not you, stupid; the real birds."

"We'll get some records," Clayton said. "The next time we're in Toronto. Birdsong records. So that next spring we'll be able to identify them." He pulled on his Aran Islands sweater over his pyjamas. Would it be cheating, he wondered, to buy an electric heater for their bedroom?

"Crows caw in units of three," Barbara said. "Caw. Caw. Caw." She inhaled. "Caw. Caw. Caw. Mrs. Perley told me. She also told me that crows hold trials. They form a circle on the ground, she said, with the crow that's been accused of a crime in the centre of it; and if they find him guilty they kill him. Her father had seen places where the crows had held court, she said. There'd be a dead crow lying there with a circle of crow tracks around it."

"That's terrific. I must ask Bob Warren in the folklore department about it."

"I'd rather you didn't."

"Why not?"

"We came here to live, remember? Not to research a dissertation on the quaint beliefs and practices of the natives."

"Purist." He touched his index finger to his lips and then to the tip of her nose. "What would you like for breakfast? I'd suggest one of Murdoch's famous omelettes."

"I'm going to be shamelessly decadent and go back to sleep. Tonight could be hectic and God knows at what unholy hour Barry will get up tomorrow."

"I think I'll take the VW into town as soon as I've had breakfast," he told her. "Collect food and drink for the multitudes."

"For the Mummers," she said. "The Mummers." She frowned, pushing out her lower lip with the tip of her tongue. "Mummers. Mummers. After you say it aloud a few times it starts to sound sinister."

He plugged in his razor; there was no outlet in the bathroom. "Any word will sound sinister if you keep repeating it.

Didn't you ever frighten yourself that way when you were a kid? I did. I'd pick a word, and say it over and over again until I almost wet my pants, I was so scared." The razor clicked and went dead. "Damn. I've blown another fuse. We're going to have to hire an electrician to go over this place from top to bottom."

"Why don't you let it grow? You looked like a nineteenth-century Russian nihilist when I met you."

"And have everyone in Butler's Crossing refer to me as that bearded weirdie professor? No, thanks." His hand was on the brass doorknob. "I'll shave in the kitchen. Like a good farmer. And don't worry about tonight. Everything will be fine."

"I'll stay here with six good men while you take the buckboard to town."

"A whole squadron would never get through, but one man flying low might make it."

She blew him a kiss.

To reach the stairs, it was necessary for him to pass through his son's room. Several of the oldest houses in Butler's Crossing, erected by men who had fought with Butler's Rangers on the losing side in the American War of Independence, were built with some of the upstairs rooms situated behind the others and without direct access to the hall. According to local legend, the object was to ensure that nubile daughters were unable to leave the house at night without waking their parents; but Clayton surmised that it was actually a matter of obtaining the maximum benefit from the available heat.

Barry slept in his Snoopy-and-the-Red-Baron pyjamas, beautiful and squalid, a golden angel with snot on its upper lip. He'd have room to grow here, where there were birches for him to swing on, and a swimming hole where he had gone skinny-dipping last summer. (The boy had been very self-conscious at first, it was so strange to strip naked outdoors and swim among darting fish). *Next year*, Clayton decided, *I'll buy him a horse.* He smiled at the thought of the heir of the lower-middle-class Murdochs riding a horse like the Queen of England's daughter.

The kitchen, larger than many apartments he had known, smelled of mint and dried apples. Through the window, across the bluish-white fields, could be seen the orchard where the apples had been picked, he and his wife and son working together, "like the old pioneers," Barry had said. Nearer the house were the chokecherry bushes from which they had gathered berries—"We must be careful to leave enough for the birds," Barbara had kept saying—to be made into a thick, sweet wine. In the living room stood the ten-foot-tall spruce he had chopped down and they had dragged home to be decorated with red and green paper streamers, Christmas cards, and popcorn balls.

Into a bowl he broke three eggs that had been laid the previous day by his own hens, brown eggs in memory of his postgraduate years in England. He stirred in three tablespoonfuls of water from his own well, white pepper, a pinch of sea salt, and two heaping tablespoonfuls of grated cheddar, made locally and sold at the weekly farmers' market in town. Two slices of homemade bread containing stone-ground wheat, an orange, and a glass of milk completed his meal, after which he took his vitamin C, vitamin E, and halibut liver oil capsules.

Barry was up. Yawning and blinking, his eyes slightly out of focus, his body and mind undergoing a child's long, slow ascent from sleep to wakefulness. "Hiyuh, guy," Clayton greeted him. "Want the old man to whip you up an omelette?"

"I'd rather have a cheeseburger," the boy said.

Clayton laughed. "You're a barbarian, do you know that?"

"What's a barbarian?"

"A barbarian is someone who eats cheeseburgers for breakfast and doesn't use his handkerchief."

"I wasn't picking my nose. I was scratching it."

"Okay. But next time use a handkerchief. How about an enormous bowl of granola and a tall glass of fresh milk from Carvell Perley's Jersey cow, unpasteurized and free of all chemical additives? There's a civilized breakfast, my son."

"Gary Armstrong picks his nose all the time," Barry said. "He's the toughest guy in Butler's Crossing."

"What makes you think that?"

"He put a guy in the hospital."

"Somebody's been kidding you."

"I was there."

"You were there?"

"Sure. All the kids were there." The boy shadowboxed. "Wham! Gary gave it to him right in the mouth. And then, wham! he gave it to him again, right in the guts. And when he got him down he kicked him. There was blood all over the place."

"Sounds to me as if you'd been watching too much television again."

"I didn't make it up. Ask anybody. Ask Bud at the diner. That's where it happened: in the yard out back."

"Are you sure you aren't exaggerating, just a little?"

"I am not exaggerating. There was blood all over the place, just like I said."

"And when did all this happen?"

"Yesterday afternoon."

"How come you didn't mention it before?"

The boy shrugged. "I don't know. Just never thought of it, I guess."

"Drink your milk."

Barry drank. "The other guy was an Indian," he said.

Oh, Lord. "Do you think that made it right?"

"Do I think what made it right?"

"Do you think it was all right for Gary Armstrong to beat up a guy just because he was an Indian?"

"No."

"Listen, guy, I want to have a talk about this with you. Later. In the meantime, let's not say anything about this to your mother. Okay?"

"Okay." Barry finished his milk and wiped his mouth on his sleeve. "I bet Gary Armstrong eats cheeseburgers for breakfast," he said.

On the way to town, Clayton listened to the news on the car radio. Killing in Ulster. Killing in Lebanon. Killing in Angola.

Killing in Eritrea. Killing in Timor. Where was Timor? The planet was a house packed with children whose parents had abandoned them. When the children were not destroying furniture or smashing windows they were at one another's throats. One day they would set the house on fire and that would be the end of it, and of them.

Back in Chicago, a neighbour of the Murdochs, the wife of a professor, had been beaten to death in her own apartment by a boy of Gary Armstrong's age: fifteen. But that was in Chicago (Shy-Cargo, they pronounced it here). There hadn't been a murder in Butler's Crossing since the 1920s. He was aware of this because people still talked about it. A MacKinnon boy had killed his girlfriend, and been hanged for it. They were both of them buried beside the Baptist church.

He stopped at Munroe's Texaco for gasoline. Graham Munroe came out to the pumps, a fat man in a black overcoat; Graham's Kosygin coat, Barbara called it. "Morning, Professor," Graham said. "A great day for tracking deer, eh?" This was hunting country. The locals killed deer and moose; Clayton could make large allowances for that—unlike Barbara, who had at first refused to cook the venison steak Graham had given them that fall—but he shared her detestation of the business executives from New York and New Jersey who flew up in their private planes to get drunk, play poker, and shoot bears.

"Would you fill it up, please, Graham?" Clayton got out, as customary in Butler's Crossing, to stand and talk with the man working the pump. "How is Florence?"

"Able to sit up and take a little nourishment." This was one of the standard local responses to such a question, an old joke. As Clayton knew, Florence Munroe was in the best of health. "How are all your folks?"

"Just fine, Graham. We're all looking forward to tonight."

"To being visited by the Mummers, you mean?" The big man returned the hose to its hanger. "It's mostly foolishness. Just a bunch of the fellows letting off steam." He glanced at the gauge on the pump. "That will be nine dollars and seventy-five cents, Professor."

Clayton accompanied Graham inside, so Graham would not have to come back with the change. The counter held display cards of Alka-Seltzer and of Gillette, Wilkinson, and Schick razor blades. "You're becoming kind of a celebrity around here," Graham said as he punched keys on an ancient cash register.

"A celebrity?"

"Everybody's talking about your committee."

"Oh, that. It's not my committee. I'm just a member. And not a very active one. I just happen to believe that it would be a bloody shame to let a pulp company pollute this valley. If they're not stopped, no one will be able to fish or swim in the river—not to mention the fact that the pulp mills stink to high heaven."

"Some folks call that the smell of money," Graham chuckled. "Hey, I almost forgot. The wife would of killed me if I hadn't given you this." He reached under the counter and came up with a package wrapped in tinfoil. "It's one of her year-old fruit cakes. She wanted you people to have it."

"I don't know what to say." Clayton pulled back a corner of the tinfoil. "My God, but it smells good." The aroma of cloves, cinnamon, raisins, currants, and brandy momentarily enveloped his mind. "Thank you, Graham, and give Florence a kiss for me."

Afterwards he wondered if that had been the right thing to say and decided that it probably hadn't been. In Butler's Crossing, certain formalities were involved in every relationship, including the most intimate ones; even the closest friends, even husbands and wives, kept a little distance between one another, always. Theirs was the better way, Clayton suspected, but it was too late in his life for him to learn to be comfortable with it. If the old girl had been there, he might actually have given her a peck on the cheek before he thought—and what an embarrassment that would have been for all three of them!

The road was a trifle slippery with powdered snow, and in the tree-shaded stretches there were patches of ice, but he had it largely to himself. Driving the twenty miles to town, he met or passed only six or seven vehicles. Most of the drivers blew their horns, flashed their headlights on and off, or waved.

He picked up his mail at the university. Invitations to New Year's parties, memos from the chairman of the department, Christmas cards from Chicago, Toronto, and London, a letter accepting a paper on D. H. Lawrence's influence on George Orwell that he had submitted to *Queen's Quarterly*, and a note from Bob Warren reminding him that they had agreed to have lunch together today at the Faculty Club.

The campus was deserted except for the few foreign students who had nowhere to go for the holidays. Next year, he resolved, he and Barbara would fill the old house with young Taiwanese and Pakistanis, give them a real old Cornelius Krieghoff kind of Christmas. Perhaps they would also invite some of their Butler's Crossing neighbours, the Perleys, Munroes, MacKinnons, Armstrongs, Davidsons, and Sinclairs. That should be fun. A gentle cultural shock for both Carvell Perley and Goordut Singh. But this year he wanted his Butler's Crossing Christmas to be without distractions; and a Butler's Crossing Christmas it was to be: tomorrow they would dine not on turkey but on chicken and roast pork, as their neighbours did.

His next stop was a shopping plaza, a staggeringly ugly purple-and-orange monstrosity flanked by a supermarket, Colonel Sanders Kentucky Fried Chicken, the Tower of Pizza, and a self-service filling station. The place reminded him of an essay he had read as an undergraduate in which H. L. Mencken argued that there was a libido for the ugly, a sensual wallowing in the hideous. Clayton supposed it was the spiritual equivalent of vandalism.

From a battery of loudspeakers there blared a recording of the Korean Orphans' Chorus singing "The Little Drummer Boy." Everything in Woolworths was made of plastic: there was plastic glass, plastic steel, plastic wood, even a fireplace made of plastic bricks and filled with plastic logs that gave off plastic flames. Still, it was apparent from the faces of the shoppers that here in this little city of one hundred thousand people, the corruption was not yet complete. Few here wore tight-lipped, flesh-coloured masks and had electromagnetic eyes. Some of them actually smiled or nodded or said things like, "Some crowd, eh?" in response to his murmured, "Pardon me," when he bumped against them.

He bought Barry a Junior TV Magician set. Barbara would disapprove. "You knew very well it would be nothing but a few scraps of cardboard and some bits of coloured plastic," she would say to Barry; and then to Clayton, "I thought we'd agreed that there'd be no store-bought presents," using the words "store-bought" to show that she wasn't really upset, although of course she was. And he would say, "This way he'll see for himself what kind of rip-off artists he'll have to deal with for the next fifty or sixty years." Then, probably, they'd laugh, and he and Barry would sit down on the floor with the set between them and he would study the directions.

In the parking lot, on his way back to his car, Clayton met Bruce MacKinnon, who owned the farm next to his. "Doin' some last-minute shoppin' are you, Professor?" the old man said. Like many farmers when they came to town, he was dressed more like an athlete on his way to a game; his sporty slacks, jacket, and cap, all of which looked as if they were being worn for the first time, were in marked contrast to his wind-burnt and mottled face, his yellowish-grey hair.

"It's a madhouse in there," Clayton said.

"Just so long as they ain't sold out of Christmas cheer," the old man said. "Thought I might slip in and buy myself a little bottle of it." He winked. "What the wife don't know won't hurt her, I always say."

"I hope we'll see you tonight," Clayton said.

"Oh, you won't see me tonight, Professor." The old man poked Clayton in the ribs as if this were the punchline of a joke he considered hilarious.

"I'm sorry to hear that," Clayton said, wondering what it was the old man found so funny.

"You won't be seein' nobody from Butler's Crossing."

"What makes you think that?"

"I don't think it, Professor. I know it. There won't be one single, solitary soul from Butler's Crossing at your place tonight."

Oh! It was part of the game. "But some other people might be visiting us, I take it?"

"Well, now, I wouldn't be surprised if you was right." The old man held out his hand. "Merry Christmas to you, Professor."

"And a very merry Christmas to you, Mr. MacKinnon."

"It's the magic of the mask," said Bob Warren, adjusting his sandwich so the smoked meat would be less likely to slip out from between the two slices of rye bread when he raised it to his mouth. "The wearer becomes the person, animal, or thing that the mask represents."

"A living folk ritual going on within twenty miles of this university. My God! Isn't it fabulous?" Clayton sipped from his glass of Dutch beer.

"You'll be disappointed, you know," Warren said. "It's pretty crude stuff. You and Barbara are expecting them to entertain you with a miracle play or some such thing. Actually, it's more like Halloween."

67

"It will be fun, anyway," Clayton said.

"They pretend not to recognize each other, of course, and that gives them a freedom they don't have at any other time. If you're not going to eat that pickle, could I have it?"

Clayton speared the pickle and transferred it to Warren's plate. "It should be interesting to see Butler's Crossing with its inhibitions down."

"It's a relatively harmless way of releasing the tensions that build up in a small, insular society. The university should devise something similar; we're another small, insular society reeking with suppressed malice."

Barry went to bed early, hoping in this way to trick the morning into coming sooner, after which Clayton went out to the woodshed and came back with the bobsled he'd had Gerrish Davidson make for the boy. "Three generations have slid down Eriskay Ridge on some of my sleds," Gerrish had said, spitting tobacco juice on the snow; and Clayton didn't doubt it. The sled was built to last, as was everything that the men and women of Butler's Crossing shaped with their hands. "This should last me out," they would say matter-of-factly of a quilt, a table, or a chair they had made, meaning that it would outlast their bodies, "and the young ones should be able to get some use out of it after I'm through with it."

"I hope he likes it," Clayton said.

"He'll love it," Barbara said. "Why wouldn't he?"

"It may turn out that he'd rather have one of those 'flying saucer' things. I've seen a lot of kids around Butler's Crossing on them, and kids his age are awfully damn imitative."

"Not Barry."

"You sound like a Jewish mother."

"All mothers are Jewish mothers."

"I'd better start making the punch."

The beverage was known to the Scots as 'het pint' and to Butler's Crossing as 'moose milk.' He warmed and thickened beer, added sugar and spices, and spiked it with Teacher's Highland Cream. "My God," Barbara said, "the smell of it alone is enough to make anyone drunk."

"I had to pry the recipe out of Graham Munroe. You'd have thought I was asking him to betray a tribal secret." He took a cautious sip. "Hey, it's not bad. Surprisingly pleasant, as a matter of fact. Here. Try it."

"Later. I don't want to plunge headfirst into the clam chowder."

"The chowder smells terrific." His lips brushed her cheek. "I think I'll put on a record. Something Christmasy."

He took down a recording of carols by Joan Baez. Adjusting the stereo set, he decided that his New Year's resolution would be to resume his guitar lessons. There were men and women here who could teach him the songs their grandparents had taught them. He also decided that during the holidays he would talk with Barbara about having another child. The world might be overpopulated, but his world wasn't. He pictured himself celebrating Christmas thirty years from now in this same house, surrounded by his grandchildren. He grinned; that is what came of drinking Graham Munroe's moose milk.

Someone knocked loudly. "Here we go," Clayton said.

Eight or ten people stood on the steps or in the walk. "Will ye let the Mummers in?" The speaker wore a black hood; as he spoke the words, he inhaled deeply. "Come in," Clayton said, remembering too late that, according to tradition, he ought to have refused them admittance at first. Hooting, stamping their feet, scattering snow everywhere, some of them beating saucepans with wooden spoons, the Mummers entered.

They smelled of mothballs and of dusty attics and airless closets. Several of the men—now that they were inside, in the light, Clayton saw that they were all men—wore women's hats and dresses. One of them elbowed him so violently that he almost fell. The elbower, who wore a red devil Halloween mask, laughed; and the others pounded their saucepans.

Barbara ladled hot punch into Irish porcelain mugs. "Do you know who I am, Professor?" demanded a man who wore a woman's stocking over his head and what looked like a nurse's cape over his shoulders.

"I'm afraid I don't," Clayton answered.

"He's afraid he don't!" Black Hood snorted.

"I thought you guys was supposed to know everything that there is to know," Stocking Head said. Clayton laughed. "Are you laughin' at me?" Stocking Head snarled.

"I'm laughing at myself," Clayton said.

"The Professor is laughin' at himself!" Stocking Head told the others. There was more beating of saucepans.

They were all of them very drunk, Clayton realized. He raised his mug and, unable to think of anything to else to say, said, "Merry Christmas!"

Nobody responded.

"You haven't told us who you are," Barbara said to Stocking Head.

"He's St. George," said Red Devil. "He's St. George and I'm Beelzebub."

Bob Warren might be right about their not remembering the old Mummers' plays, but at least they had not forgotten two of the stock characters.

"I rescue fair ladies in distress," said Stocking Head. "Tell me, fair lady, are you in distress?"

"I hope not," Barbara said.

"She hopes not," said the others, inhaling on the first word and exhaling on the last two. Red Devil was not the only one to wear a Halloween mask; there was also Dracula, Frankenstein's monster, and what Clayton guessed to be the Phantom of the Opera. Yet they didn't look in the least silly, these muscular drunken men.

"Drink up, Professor," said Beelzebub, whom Clayton had by now identified as Graham Munroe. Clayton drank. If he kept this up, he would turn into a sleepwalker.

"Stop that, damn it!" Barbara said. There was a roar of lewd laughter. Shaking the fog out of his eyes, Clayton saw that Stocking Head's hands were under her sweater.

"Hey, come on now," Clayton said to Stocking Head, who called himself St. George and spoke with Gary Armstrong's voice. *The dumb kid!* he thought. Yet the others weren't laughing good-naturedly at the boy; they were laughing derisively at Barbara. He could single out the shrill cackle of old Bruce McKinnon.

"You like to tease, don't you, fair lady?" Gary Armstrong said. "Runnin' around with no bra. Just beggin' for it."

"The joke has gone far enough, Gary," Clayton said.

"I bet she don't wear no pants either!" cackled old MacKinnon from the sanctuary of his black hood.

"Do you wear panties, Barbara?" said Graham Munroe, safe in the armour of Beelzebub.

"Come on, guys," Clayton said, "let's all have another drink."

"Listen to the great professor!" said Beelzebub. "The great professor that has been doin' his damndest to keep us from gettin' our pulp mill."

So that accounted for their rancour. "It's Christmas, Graham," Clayton said.

"He thinks we don't know it's Christmas!" Beelzebub said. There was a great pounding of saucepans. In a remote corner of his consciousness, Clayton registered the fact that Dracula had thrown a burning cigarette butt on the floor and was crushing it out with his heel.

"There will be some pretty lean Christmases on Eriskay Ridge if him and his committee get their way," somebody said.

"It's not my committee," Clayton said.

"Him and his committee!" old MacKinnon said. "They don't like the smell of sulphur. They'll smell plenty of it in hell."

More laughter, more pounding of saucepans. Somebody staggered against the table; there was the sound of breaking glass.

"I want you people to get out of my house," Barbara said.

"Darling," Clayton said.

"Clayton, I want these people out of my house. What kind of a Christmas is this?" She began to cry. "Damn!" she said. He knew how she despised herself when she cried. "Damn!" she said again.

Suddenly, the Mummers were silent; and just as suddenly, Clayton was angry. Afterwards he was to reflect uncomfortably that he might not have been so vehement if their silence had not freed him from his fear of them. For he had been afraid.

"Goddamn it," he said. There was a shuffling of heavily booted feet. "We thought you people were our friends." Nobody spoke. "We thought we had found a home here." *Oh dear God*, he thought, *keep me from crying too.*

"You don't understand, Professor," Graham Munroe said. He had taken off his mask.

"For Christ's sake, stop calling me 'Professor'!"

"Clayton, you don't understand. We're the Mummers. We act the fool this way in every house in the settlement."

"Like hell," Clayton said.

"I swear to God. A little farther down the road, we'll be giving somebody the devil for being in favour of the pulp mill. Oh, maybe young Gary went a little farther with your missus than he would of gone with Bruce MacKinnon's old woman." There was uncertain laughter. "But he didn't mean any harm. He thought she'd get a laugh out of it. And as far as the stuff we said to you goes—my God, man, that was mild compared to some of the things we've said to other people."

"We didn't treat you folks one damn bit different than we'd treat anybody else," old MacKinnon said. "Except we wasn't as hard on you. And that's the God's truth."

"The boys wouldn't of stopped here if it hadn't been for me," Carvell Perley said. His tone was apologetic. "We don't usually bother strangers."

They left quietly with murmured goodnights, still drunk but no longer the Mummers. Clayton helped Barbara clean up the cigarette butts and broken glass.

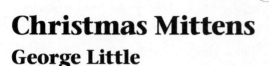

Christmas Mittens
George Little

The man lurching up the crowded bus couldn't always have been old. But to Jenny Anderson, something about him had been old for a long, long time. As he crushed in beside her, she tried to keep the gift-wrapped parcels on her knee away from him. To tell the truth, he was dirty and smelled of stale sweat and cheap wine.

He might be about the age of her father, seventy-five or so, but it was hard to tell. He might be younger, for his age would have little to do with the number of years he had lived. When she compared him with her father, there were no other points of reference she could use. After her dad's retirement only five years before, he had kept active in volunteer work with Meals on Wheels and, at this time of the year, with the Christmas Basket Appeal. That was until he started to be forgetful a few months ago and the doctor wouldn't let him drive anymore.

The man beside her stared without seeing at the back of the seat ahead of him; there was no spark, no smile, nothing of the vitality that had marked her father's expressive face. She tried not to resent him for not being like her dad, for not having made anything of his life. If only her dad still had his memory, he would be out there being useful; he wouldn't just give up.

The man's dirty brown coat, its greasy collar pulled up around his scrawny neck, his ragged dress pants of the kind

75

sold at rummage sales, and his thin grey shoes only reminded her of her father's neatness. He had always worn a stiff collar and neatly knotted tie to work, and in retirement he kept the habit.

When she went to visit him in his meticulous apartment, he always met her at the door with a hug, enveloping her in a faint atmosphere of Old Spice and talcum powder. And when he stood back, he was always dressed neatly—pants pressed, shoes polished, collar and tie as sharp as when he was in the accounts office where he had worked for nearly fifty years.

He had always been an independent man, and he cared for himself better than she would have done, if he had let her. In the senior citizens' complex, where he had moved after her mother died three years ago, he appeared happy and sufficient. His failing memory was the only cause for concern he gave her; she worried that he would leave the stove on and start a fire.

The old man next to her nodded sharply to ward off sleep. Feeling her flinch against his leaning body, he turned to her in apology.

"Sorry, Miss, eh? Stuffy in here."

She returned his bleary smile, but weakly enough, she hoped, to discourage any further conversation. He did speak, but not to her, nor to anyone in particular.

"God, I hate Christmas. People with too many parcels, bus too crowded; should take cabs. I always used to take a cab, myself. Too dear now, too damn dear. Hate the whole thing." He raised his hand to wipe a drip from the end of his thin nose. A dirty thumb and dirtier thumbnail showed through a gaping hole in his red mitten. "Pick up my cheque today, buy my presents. Still got a day before it's Christmas, plenty time. Don't know what to get Margie, new gloves maybe, if they're not too much. That's what she would like anyways, Margie."

The parcels on her knee suddenly became heavier, but in spite of herself, she spoke to him. "Is Margie your wife?"

He tried to focus his eyes on her, as though her face was too near. "Wife? God no, she's my neighbour, lives in the next room, up the North End. Not well, you know, lungs bad. Heart too, they say at the clinic."

He looked away from her again and lifted his grubby mitt to rub some graffiti off the seatback in front of him. "Used to be married, though...me, not Margie. Then she left me, took the kids too. Can't blame her, eh? No good drunk—now, not before. Never could keep a job, after the trouble in the office. Never think, eh? I used to work in an office—accountant, good money."

Jenny stiffened and looked at his profile, watching tears brim his eyes. "What firm were you with? Wasn't Barnes and Williams, was it?" Please God, it couldn't have been her father's old firm.

"No, nothing that posh—small outfit, down Dock Street. Closed down ten, fifteen years ago."

She felt relieved, although she didn't know why. Having found her point of reference, it was no comfort. The discovered similarity between this stranger and her father merely widened the obvious gap between the two men, the two worlds.

Her stop, the one nearest her dad's apartment block, came before his. She fought with herself whether to offer him money before she left, but at last decided she didn't know how without making a fuss. He rose shakily, but with a kind of grand politeness, to let her pass. "Have a nice Christmas, Miss," he called after her.

"You too," she called back.

As the bus drew away, she noticed that he had moved up to the window seat; but when she gave him a half wave with the hand holding her purse, he did not respond. He was busy rubbing the back of the seat in front of him with the thumb that showed through his mitten.

The building where her dad lived had once been the city's finest hotel. In the lobby, which still retained some of the grandeur of the old hotel, she buzzed apartment 204, noticing how neatly her father had printed his name, John Whiting, in italic script beside the button.

She waited for her father's answer on the intercom, expecting him to play his usual game of pretending not to know who she was and demanding impossible identification before he buzzed to open the inner door. To her surprise, he buzzed right away without even asking who she was, a clear breach of the building's security code. As she pushed the door open with her shoulder and made her way to the elevator, she was vaguely worried that something was wrong.

When her father opened the door of 204 and she kissed him briefly on the cheek, her unease grew. He looked unfinished, as though someone else had dressed him and hadn't got it quite right. He was wearing his usual collar and tie and pressed pants, but it looked somehow like yesterday's neatness. The bottom three buttons on his Fair Isle cardigan were undone, and his wispy white hair had not been brushed as carefully as usual.

She put her bag down on the counter that separated the tiny kitchen from the living room, and took off her fur hat and heavy sheepskin coat. He made no effort to play the part of footman as he usually did, standing by in mock servility to hold her coat for her as she struggled out of her long, fur-lined boots. When she came back from hanging up her things, he was sitting by the window, looking out. The window looked out over the square; he did not seem to be looking anywhere.

"You okay, Dad? Nothing wrong, is there?" She sat in what had been her mother's favourite chair in the old house, a firm wing-backed armchair with low arms, a good knitting chair. "I see you started putting up the decorations." Started, she thought, but not finished.

There was one faded Christmas bell hanging from the archway, the one they had always hung above the kitchen door at home, and a string of tarnished tinsel hung from one thumb tack, waiting to be stretched along the wall and pinned in place. There was a big box of fairy lights and ornaments by the television, with a green tangle of cords and plugs dangling over the side.

"Come on, I'll help you finish." He roused himself then, and for a time they were busy trying to make the cramped room look Christmasy.

"Remember when I made this pipe-cleaner Santa Claus?" she said, pulling a bedraggled ornament from the box. "It was always the last thing Mum put on the tree every year. And look at this, I remember where we got this—Santa's Village—one summer when I was about six. Remember, you told me it was Christmas all year round there, and I wondered why we couldn't stay instead of driving on to Montreal." Jenny put the tiny china reindeer on top of the mahogany bookshelves.

From under the mess of lights and cords, he lifted a cardboard box and opened it. "What's this?" he asked. "I don't remember this." It was a carved wooden nativity scene with wise men and shepherds kneeling before Mary and Joseph and the Christ child. On the stable roof, a star glittered.

"You made this, Dad. Don't you remember, before I was born; you used to touch the paint up every year. Mum always put it on the mantle with pine boughs around it. It was her favourite thing."

When she looked at him for confirmation, he was staring out the window. "Oh yes," he said, "that was it. But who are all the people in there? That's a baby. What's it doing there? I should know that, shouldn't I, Jenny?" He was weeping silently as Jenny took the box from his hands and sat down beside him on the couch.

He had told her the story—her very own, made up just for her—every Christmas Eve until she was eleven or twelve; now she told it to him. Each time, he had told her the whole story, for she would have objected if he had missed out even the slightest detail. Now, sitting beside him, holding his hands—clean hands that even with their neatly trimmed nails seemed suddenly old—she wove the tale again in his own words, words that came back to her effortlessly, like those childhood prayers imprinted on the memory; they return to the mind years after you have forgotten you ever learned them, quite unbidden and in surprising exactness.

The angels, the shepherds in the fields, the young wife and the older husband, the baby in the manger, and the little girl he had always built into his version of the story, who knitted a pair of tiny mittens to bring to the baby Jesus. He sat and listened, his face as full of wonder as she knew hers must have been when she heard the story for the first time. "I think I remember it now," he said, when she finished with the bit about the girl getting to hold the baby, and him smiling up into her face and holding her thumb with his little fist. "And that girl, she was you, wasn't she, Jenny? Yes, she was you."

He seemed much brighter before she left, and had even made her scrambled eggs and toast for tea. She told him she would be round the next morning with Bill and the boys to take him to church, and then home to their place for dinner.

On the way down the elevator, she thought how Dad had always been central to their Christmases, writing rhymes for the labels of her gifts and her mother's, making sure things were done right. She fought back tears when she remembered how she had to tell him his own story.

When she stepped out of the lobby, the street lights were on and the trees in the square were twinkling with coloured lights.

From loudspeakers near the tall Christmas tree by the office building down the street, she could hear a choir singing "O Holy Night."

As she walked down the street, holding her coat collar up around her face against the biting wind, she thought of the other man, the man on the bus who hated Christmas, the man with the mittens. And she made herself a promise that she and Bill would seek him out after Christmas and see what they could do to help him. She didn't know where he was, but she felt a deep need to find him.

The Celluloid Angel
Jennifer Wade

I t was an unusually snowy Christmas season in Fredericton when the celluloid angel came into our house. All afternoon of that Christmas Eve day, the flakes grew thicker and thicker as they whirled around the Salvation Army man ringing his bell on Queen Street.

It was because of the snow that my mother took a shortcut through the department store to the parking lot. But as she made her way through the aisles filled with last-minute shoppers, she suddenly stopped in front of the Christmas ornaments arranged haphazardly in bins.

"Look at the perfect face on that angel—a totally perfect face."

She pointed to a cream-coloured celluloid angel upended in one of the bins. Although it was more expensive than all the other half-priced ornaments, we were to have it; the last Christmas purchase, it was placed on top of already overflowing bags.

We drove home slowly in the Christmas whiteness that now covered the old stone church on Brunswick Street, the snow that was settling on the verandas of the large old homes and dimming the brightness of Christmas lights around the front porches. My mother said little as we passed the snow-covered benches, the lampposts, and the wading pool in Wilmot Park. Across the road, the grand lines of the RCMP headquarters were also being softened by the falling snow; beyond the magnificence of that building, whiteness covered the dark of the St. John River.

"That's a perfect face," my mother breathed, "the kind of face that Italian painters for centuries have painted—perfect, so very perfect."

She was talking less to me than to herself, but I knew she was referring to the angel.

When we reached home, my father appeared in the kitchen with his newspaper and asked where we had been, as though the many bags of goods did not themselves give answer.

"You must see what we got for the front window," my mother answered as she unwrapped the angel. She turned on a little switch to light the taper that the angel held in front of her. Immediately, shadows fell softly over the pale face, and the high-arched brows gave it a sense of wonder.

In the glow of the light, my mother spoke with quiet reverence. "It's lovely."

That was enough to launch my father into delivery of his Christmas message: the waste, the spending, the nonsense, the frippery; where was more junk going to be stored? And were there not already too many ornaments in the house? And why had my mother impetuously invited total strangers for Christmas dinner? Wasn't our own family quite large enough?

There was no stopping him now. Most of this we had heard before. To be exact, we had heard it every Christmas Eve for as long as I could remember. Only the occasion of the delivery changed. Then he asked my mother the question that changed the mood that Christmas: "Why did you get this celluloid department-store thing with painted golden wings?" My mother did not answer, but began slowly to slice a ham for supper.

Evening and darkness had descended. It was Christmas Eve. I stared at the pink flush on the angel's pale face. The eyes seemed to be averted, not looking at the glow of her taper, but wistfully aside.

Outside, the snow kept falling—falling on the cemetery across the road where Jake Thompson had been buried after a duck-hunting accident on one of the islands in the river; the cemetery where Steve Lang's little sister lay in a grave with a carved lamb on top of it; the cemetery where two executed brothers had been buried; the cemetery where wooden crosses marked the graves of German soldiers who had died far from home. The snow evened and whitened all the graves.

I was away for many Christmases after that one. Each year, as far as I know, the little angel was lit and put among the pine sprays on the front window ledge, and each year I was told that someone had remarked on the delicacy of the face; and each year, I am sure, my father found Christmas more of an intrusion and participated less and less.

When my mother died, the house was to be sold. A lot of what my father had referred to as junk was given away. Most of the Christmas ornaments that had accumulated through the years went in a box to the Salvation Army. Only some bells, a wreath my mother had made, and the angel remained.

In that year of change, an earthy woman called Ruthie, a woman full of good sense and little humour, came to keep house for my father. Ruthie was hardly the diminutive being her name would suggest, and I rather think my father feared her.

That Christmas was subdued; there was no snow. It was a difficult one for my father. On Christmas Eve, there was no tirade now to cast a pall over any magic. I wrapped gifts on the kitchen table. On the radio, a choir was singing from somewhere in Saskatchewan.

Through the doorway I could see my father leaning on the mantelpiece, sipping a brandy and staring into the fire. Then I watched him cross the room to the china cupboard. He reached in and brought out the celluloid angel from behind the blue Confederation plate. For a moment he looked at it, and then he turned on the little light at the end of the taper that had been held steadfastly in the clasped hands of the angel all these years. The ivory of the gown had yellowed, one of the golden wings was chipped, but the face, I thought, looked softer and sweeter than ever.

Once more the little angel was put on the window ledge against the darkness of the night, and my father returned to the fireplace.

Ruthie came to help me set the table and to tell me what else needed to be done for this last Christmas in the old house.

"Ain't that queer he'd get that old thing and put it up there?" she asked, as she looked at the angel.

My father overheard her and turned around. Sheepishly, she laughed. "That sure is an old ornament. Looks as if she's havin' a smoke with that light out in front of her. "

For the first time, I noticed that my father had aged since my mother's death.

"You know, Ruthie," he said, "two men looked through prison bars. One saw mud; the other, stars."

Turning away from the angel that glowed against the night, he rubbed the corner of his eye with one finger, and went to put another log on the fire.

Ruthie shrugged. "Your father sure is a funny man," she said.

On the kitchen radio, the choir in Saskatchewan was zestfully singing the last refrain of "O Come, All Ye Faithful."

A Christmas Mistake
Lucy Maud Montgomery

"Tomorrow is Christmas," announced Teddy Grant exultantly, as he sat on the floor struggling manfully with a refractory bootlace that was knotted and tagless and stubbornly refused to go into the eyelets of Teddy's patched boots. "Ain't I glad, though. Hurrah!"

His mother was washing the breakfast dishes in a dreary, listless sort of way. She looked tired and broken-spirited. Ted's enthusiasm seemed to grate on her, for she answered sharply:

"Christmas indeed. I can't see that it is anything for us to rejoice over. Other people may be glad enough; but what with winter coming on, I'd sooner it was spring than Christmas. Mary Alice, do lift that child out of the ashes and put its shoes and stockings on. Everything seems to be at sixes and sevens here this morning."

Keith, the oldest boy, was coiled up on the sofa calmly working out some algebra problems, quite oblivious to the noise around him. But he looked up from his slate, with his pencil suspended above an obstinate equation, to declaim with a flourish:

"Christmas comes but once a year,

And then mother wishes it wasn't here."

"I don't then," said Gordon, son number two, who was preparing his own noon lunch of bread and molasses at the table, and making an atrocious mess of crumbs and sugary syrup over everything, "and that is that there'll be no school. We'll have a whole week of holidays."

Gordon was noted for his aversion to school and his affection for holidays.

"And we're going to have turkey for dinner," declared Teddy, getting up off the floor and rushing to secure his share of bread and molasses, "and cranb'ry sauce and—and—pound cake! Ain't we, ma?"

"No, you are not," said Mrs. Grant desperately, dropping the dishcloth and snatching the baby on her knee to wipe the crust of cinders and molasses from the chubby pink-and-white face. "You may as well know it now, children, I've kept it from you so far in hopes that something would turn up, but nothing has. We can't have any Christmas dinner tomorrow—we can't afford it. I've pinched and saved every way I could for the last month hoping that I'd be able to get a turkey for you anyhow, but you'll have to do without it. There's that doctor's bill to pay and a dozen other bills coming in—and people say they can't wait. I suppose they can't, but it's kind of hard, I must say."

The little Grants stood with open mouths and horrified eyes. No turkey for Christmas! Was the world coming to an end? Wouldn't the government interfere if anyone ventured to dispense with Christmas celebration?

The gluttonous Teddy stuffed his fists into his eyes and lifted up his voice. Keith, who understood better than the others the look on his mother's face, took his blubbering younger brother by the collar and marched him into the porch. The twins, seeing this summary proceeding, swallowed the outcries they had intended to make, although they couldn't keep a few big tears from running down their fat cheeks.

Mrs. Grant looked pityingly at the disappointed faces about her.

"Don't cry, children, you make me feel worse. We are not the only ones who will have to do without a Christmas turkey. We ought to be very thankful that we have anything to eat at all. I hate to disappoint you, but it can't be helped."

"Never mind, mother," said Keith comfortingly, relaxing his hold upon the porch door, whereupon it suddenly flew open and precipitated Teddy, who had been tugging at the handle, heels-over-head backwards. "We know you've done your best. It's been a hard year for you. Just wait, though. I'll soon be grown up, and then you and these greedy youngsters shall feast on turkey every day of the year. Hello, Teddy, have you got on your feet again? Mind, sir, no more blubbering!"

"When I'm a man," announced Teddy, with dignity, "I'd just like to see you put me in the porch. And I mean to have turkey all the time and I won't give you any either."

"All right, you greedy small boy. Only take yourself off to school now, and let me hear no more squeaks out of you. Tramp, all of you, all of you, and give Mother a chance to get her work done."

Mrs. Grant got up and fell to work at her dishes with a brighter face.

"Well, we mustn't give in, perhaps things will be better after a while. I'll make a famous bread pudding, and you can boil some molasses taffy and ask those little Smithsons next door to help you pull it. They won't whine for turkey, I'll be bound. I don't suppose they ever tasted such a thing in all their lives. If I could afford it, I'd have had them all in to dinner with us. That sermon Mr. Evans preached last Sunday kind of stirred me up. He said we ought always to try and share our Christmas joy with some poor souls who had never learned the meaning of the word. I can't do as much as I'd like to. It was different when your father was alive."

The noisy group grew silent, as they always did when their father was spoken of. He had died the year before, and since his death the little family had had a hard time. Keith, to hide his feelings, began to hector the rest.

"Mary Alice, do hurry up. Here, you twin nuisances, get off to school. If you don't, you'll be late, and then the master will give you a whipping."

"He won't," asserted the irrepressible Teddy. "He never whips us, he doesn't. He stands us on the floor sometimes, though," he added, remembering the many times his own chubby legs had been seen to better advantage on the school platform.

"That man," said Mrs. Grant, alluding to the teacher, "makes me nervous. He is the most abstracted creature I ever saw in my life. It is a wonder to me he doesn't walk straight into the river someday. You'll meet him meandering along the street, gazing into vacancy, and he'll never see you nor hear a word you say half the time."

"Yesterday," said Gordon, chuckling over the remembrance, "he came in with a big piece of paper he'd picked up on the entry floor in one hand and his hat in the other—and he stuffed his hat into the coal scuttle and hung up the paper on a nail, as grave as you please. Never knew the difference till Ned Slocum went and told him. He's always doing things like that."

Keith had collected his books, and now marched his brothers and sisters off to school. Left alone with the baby, Mrs. Grant betook herself to her work with a heavy heart. But a second interruption broke the progress of her dishwashing.

"I declare," she said, with a surprised glance through the window, "if there isn't that absent-minded schoolteacher coming through the yard! What can he want! Dear me, I do hope Teddy hasn't been cutting capers in school again."

For the teacher's last call had been in October and had been occasioned by the fact that the irrepressible Teddy would persist in going to school with his pockets filled with live crickets and in driving them, harnessed to strings, up and down the aisle when the teacher's back was turned. All mild methods of punishment having failed, the teacher had called to talk it over with Mrs. Grant, with the happy result that Teddy's behaviour had improved—in the matter of crickets, at least.

But it was about time for another outbreak. Teddy had been unnaturally good for too long a time. Poor Mrs. Grant feared that it was the calm before the storm, and it was with nervous haste that she went to the door and greeted the young teacher.

He was a slight, pale, boyish-looking fellow, with an abstracted, musing look in his large dark eyes. Mrs. Grant noticed with amusement that he wore a white straw hat in spite of the season. His eyes were directed to her face with his usual unseeing gaze.

"Just as though he was looking through me at something a thousand miles away," said Mrs. Grant afterwards. "I believe he was, too. His body was right there on the step before me, but where his soul was is more than you or I or anybody can tell."

"Good morning," he said absently. "I have just called on my way to school with a message from Miss Millar. She wants you all to come up and have Christmas dinner with her tomorrow."

"For the land's sake!" said Mrs. Grant, blankly. "I don't—understand."

To herself, she thought, *I wish I dared take him and shake him to find if he's walking in his sleep or not.*

"You and all the children—everyone," the teacher went on dreamily, as if he were reciting a lesson learned beforehand. "She told me to tell you to be sure and come. Shall I say that you will?"

"Oh, yes, that is—I suppose—I don't know," said Mrs. Grant incoherently. "I never expected—yes, you may tell her we'll come," she concluded abruptly.

"Thank you," said the abstracted messenger, gravely lifting his hat and looking squarely through Mrs. Grant into unknown regions. When he had gone, Mrs. Grant went in and sat down, laughing in a sort of hysterical way.

"I wonder if it is all right. Could Cornelia really have told him? She must, I suppose, but it is enough to take one's breath."

Mrs. Grant and Cornelia Millar were cousins, and had once been the closest of friends; but that was years ago, before some spiteful reports and ill-natured gossip had come between them, making only a little rift at first that soon widened into a chasm of coldness and alienation. Therefore, this invitation surprised Mrs. Grant greatly.

Miss Cornelia was a maiden lady of certain years, with a comfortable bank account and a handsome, old-fashioned house on the hill behind the village. She always boarded the school-teachers and looked after them maternally; she was an active church worker, and a tower of strength to struggling ministers and their families.

"If Cornelia has seen fit at last to hold out the hand of reconciliation, I'm glad enough to take it. Dear knows, I've wanted to make up often enough but didn't think she ever would. We've both of us got too much pride and stubbornness. It's the Turner blood in us that does it. The Turners were all so set. But I mean to do my part now she has done hers."

And Mrs. Grant made a final attack on the dishes with a beaming face.

When the little Grants came home and heard the news, Teddy stood on his head to express his delight, the twins kissed each other, and Mary Alice and Gordon danced around the kitchen.

Keith thought himself too big to betray any joy over a Christmas dinner; but he whistled while doing the chores until the bare maples in the yard rang, and Teddy, in spite of unheard-of misdemeanours, was not collared off into the porch once.

A Christmas Mistake

When the young teacher got home from school that evening, he found the yellow house full of all sorts of delectable odours. Miss Cornelia herself was concocting mince pies after the famous family recipe, while her ancient and faithful handmaiden, Hannah, was straining into moulds the cranberry jelly. The open pantry door revealed a tempting array of Christmas delicacies. "Did you call and invite the Smithsons up to dinner as I told you?" asked Miss Cornelia anxiously.

"Yes," was the dreamy response as he glided through the kitchen and vanished into the hall.

Miss Cornelia crimped the edges of her pies delicately with a relieved air. "I made certain he'd forget it," she said. "You just have to watch him as if he were a mere child. Didn't I catch him yesterday starting off to school in his carpet slippers? And in spite of me, he got away today in that ridiculous summer hat. You'd better set that jelly in that out-pantry to cool, Hannah. It looks good. We'll give those poor little Smithsons a feast for once in their lives, if they never got another." At this juncture the hall door flew open and Mr. Palmer appeared on the threshold. He seemed considerably agitated, and for once his eyes had lost their look of space-searching.

"Miss Millar, I am afraid I did make a mistake this morning—it has just dawned on me. I am almost sure that I called at Mrs. Grant's and invited her and her family instead of the Smithsons. And she said they would come."

Miss Cornelia's face was a study.

"Mr. Palmer," she said, flourishing her crimping fork

tragically, "do you mean to say you went and invited Linda Grant here tomorrow? Linda Grant, of all women in this world!"

"I did," said the teacher with penitent wretchedness. "It was very careless of me—I am very sorry. What can I do? I'll go down and tell them I made a mistake if you like."

"You can't do that," groaned Miss Cornelia, sitting down and wrinkling up her forehead in dire perplexity. "It would never do in the world. For pity's sake, let me think for a minute."

Miss Cornelia did think—to good purpose, evidently, for her forehead smoothed out as her meditations proceeded, and her face brightened. Then she got up briskly. "Well, you've done it and no mistake. I don't know that I'm sorry, either. Anyhow, we'll leave it as it is. But you must go straight down now and invite the Smithsons too. And for pity's sake, don't make any more mistakes."

When he had gone, Miss Cornelia opened her heart to Hannah.

"I never could have done it myself—never; the Turner is too strong in me. But I'm glad it is done. I've been wanting for years to make up with Linda. And now the chance has come, thanks to that blessed, blundering boy, I mean to make the most of it. Linda must never know. Poor Linda! She's had a hard time. Hannah, we must make some more pies; and I must go straight down to the store and get some more Santa Claus stuff; I've only got enough to go around the Smithsons."

When Mrs. Grant and her family arrived at the yellow house the next morning, Miss Cornelia herself ran out bareheaded to meet them. The two women shook hands a little stiffly, and then a rill of long-repressed affection trickled out from some secret spring in Miss Cornelia's heart and she kissed her new-found old friend tenderly. Linda returned the kiss warmly and both felt that the old-time friendship was theirs again.

The little Smithsons all came, and they and the little Grants sat down in the long, bright dining room to a dinner that made history in their small lives, and was eaten over again in happy dreams for months.

How those children did eat! And how beaming Miss Cornelia and grimfaced, soft-hearted Hannah and often the absent-minded teacher himself enjoyed watching them!

After dinner Miss Cornelia distributed among the delighted little souls the presents she had bought for them, and then turned them loose in the big, shining kitchen to have a taffy pull—and they had it to their hearts' content! And as for the shocking, taffyfied state into which they got their own rosy faces and that once-immaculate domain—well, as Miss Cornelia and Hannah never said one word about it, neither will I.

The four women enjoyed the afternoon in their own way, and the schoolteacher buried himself in algebra to his own great satisfaction.

When her guests went home in the starlit December dusk, Miss Cornelia walked part of the way with them and had a long, confidential talk with Mrs. Grant. When she returned, it was to find Hannah groaning in soul over the kitchen and the schoolteacher dreamily trying to clean some molasses off his boots with the kitchen hairbrush. Long-suffering Miss Cornelia rescued her property and dispatched Mr. Palmer into the woodshed to find the shoe brush. Then she sat down and laughed.

"Hannah, what will become of that boy yet. There's no counting on what he'll do next. I don't know how he'll ever get through the world, I'm sure, but I'll look after him while he's here at least. I owe him a huge debt of gratitude for this Christmas blunder. What an awful mess this place is in! But, Hannah, did you ever in the world see anything so delightful as that little Tommy Smithson stuffing himself with plum cake, not to mention Teddy Grant? It did me good just to see them."

Christmas Memories

The Winter House
Gary L. Saunders

I can see our winter house now, its warm bulk muffled in the snowbanks of my Newfoundland childhood. I can see the golden gleam of its small windows against the February dusk. I can see the dark wall of spruce rising behind it to the cold stars, and trace the vagaries of spark showers from the stovepipe whenever a junk turns in the fire.

Standing outside our winter house in memory, I can hear things too. My mother is drawing water from the barrel in the porch: *splash* goes the dipper; *thunk* the lid. Then the table resumes its rhythmic squeak as she returns to kneading bread. The droning voice is the Gerald S. Doyle radio bulletin recounting tonight's war news. The raucous snore-and-wheeze is my grandfather enjoying his rocking chair.

We called it a winter house because it was where we lived in winter, to keep warm. Our real house, the summer house, was too chilly for winter habitation. It had sawdust under the clapboards everywhere, but still the wind sighed in here and there, circumventing the mats and blankets that my father stuffed under doors and along sills on bitter nights. One summer he fetched stout logs, did a lot of chopping and chinking, and built the winter house. That fall, we moved in. The happiest winters of my childhood followed.

Some would have called it a log cabin, I suppose. On the outside, it was. But inside was a home, and a spacious one too. We had a big kitchen–living room, three bedrooms, a pantry, and a porch. The doors inside made never a sound, for they were of smoky cotton. Green sheathing paper cozied the walls and echoed summer. An Ideal cookstove cheered the nights. Lamplight mellowed all.

"Tea time...." My mother's treble call, finding us playing somewhere in the snowscape at dusk, meant the real end of day; a vespers bell ringing me home after sunset, night by night. In the porch, the sweeping ritual proceeded, and the day's snow flew like water when a wet dog shakes himself. But the caked snow was often too tenacious for broom or brush and had to be plucked from my clothes like feathers from a chicken, until the mat would be dotted with these wool-whiskered knobs.

Supper was by lamplight in our winter house, for the days were already short when we left the summer house each November. There is magic in an old lamp. Ours was handsome whether lighted or not; but set in its bracket over the table, its lambent flame seized and amplified by the silvered reflector and beamed about the room, it seemed that no chandelier could surpass it. My mother polished the fluted chimney each morning with a page from the *Family Herald* or the *Toronto Weekly Star*. The sound she made was like frosty snow underfoot. She would fill the bowl with kerosene, snip-snip the wick into shape, and set the lamp on high again.

I smile to recall the potato she kept over the oil-can spout.

Moose, caribou, and rabbit, our fresh meat in winter, often steamed on the supper plates along with potatoes, turnips, carrots, or cabbage from the cellar. Salt beef was the standby—and still seems to me the only proper flavouring for potatoes. (I have friends who differ with me on this point, but I once converted a Danish forester.)

To wake to the smell and sound of caribou steaks and onions frying in pork fat on a winter morning beats bacon and eggs and coffee altogether, especially when you are nine years old. It's a good breakfast to go to school and learn arithmetic on. It seems disloyal to say so, but I always fancied Dad could fry wild meat better than Mom. He thought so too.

Perhaps it was natural that he should be able to, since in those days he was a trapper. Every month he made the round of his traplines, and one of my most colourful mental images is that of my father readying sled and dogs for that trek. For a week before, Mom would roll out bread and buns until there were enough. At last, when everything was aboard and lashed fast—traps, axe, kettle, and pot; bread, butter, and beans; tea, sugar, molasses, and fat pork; snowshoes and the rest—then the eager dogs would be slipped into their harnesses. A melee of yelps by the porch door, a crunch of ice and squeak of frozen wood, and he would be off. We would wave, then turn and go to school. Mom would wave, then turn and be father and mother for a few weeks.

His homecomings were just as memorable. Usually they were after dark, but as soon as we heard panting dogs, we knew who it was. Before the sleigh was halted, we would burst out, and for me the special memory is one of smell and touch: fir boughs and woodsmoke and rough, scrubbing-brush whiskers. And afterwards, a little cloth bag of spruce gum would be mine.

The Winter House

Christmases in the winter house were the best of any. I still believed in a red-jacketed Santa Claus then. One December, only a few nights before Christmas Eve, I was not behaving very well. I was advised that Saint Nick gave no gifts to naughty boys, and that at that selfsame moment he might be flying by on his reindeer, making his last-minute check on good boys and bad.

Suddenly our snow-blanketed roof came alive with the trampling of little hooves—and my parents heard them too! I raced to bed and burrowed deep.

And the hoof-prints were there the next morning—partly snowed out, but unmistakable—everywhere dimpling the low roof. But over at the northwest corner was a curious thing: two sets of tracks led off onto a high snowbank, meandered to the level snow, and ended at the barn. Now, we kept goats...and it was not hard to deduce how the two frisky animals, escaping their pen in the night, took advantage of the low eaves and high, hard-packed snowdrift to try their climbing skills.

Believing it was the hard part.

That was the Christmas I got the red sleigh. Or rather, it was the Christmas I learned Santa answered letters. In reply to my scrawly note, he left a scrawly one of his own:

Dear Gary:

Your red sleigh will come on the steamer next week.

Love,
Santa

I was bursting with pride, I remember. He, Santa Claus, *had written that note with my pencil, and on paper out of my scribbler.* I knew this because I had heard him rummaging in my book bag, which was hung on the post of my bunk, very early on Christmas morning—and had discovered that the page missing in my yellow scribbler and the page with the note were *one and the same.*

Another cause for pride was that this wonderful Father Christmas always took time to enjoy a glass of milk and slab of chocolate cake at our table, year by year. It was some time before I noted the connection between this and my father's fondness for the same snack.

One week and one day afterwards, when there was ice forming in the bay, the steamer arrived on her last trip for the season with freight for my grandfather's general store. Atop the jumble of bedsprings and onion sacks in the scow as it neared the wharf was something scarlet and gold that glinted in the sunlight. When it got close enough, I could read the magic inscription: Rocker Racer. The battered sled my father had made lay unused and dusty in the woodshed afterwards.

One winter it snowed a great deal. It snowed till every fence was erased from the landscape, and did not cease until every tree and house seemed half-submerged in a white flood. The Christmas our goats climbed onto the roof was green compared to it. Or so it seems. When the sky got blue again, our winter house was eaves-deep in the whiteness.

Men had to come and dig us out—although I would have let things remain as they were. At breakfast there came a scratching

at the snow-crusted pane: someone's mittened hand was clearing
a path for the daylight. At the same time, we heard a scraping and
grunting outside the porch: that was my portly grandfather shov-
elling into the great breakers of snow that walled us in. We could
picture him, and we smiled in spite of our plight, for Grandpa
shovelled snow in a manner all his own. Straight over his left
shoulder would fly each charge, accompanied by a grunt. It was
dangerous to stand behind him at such times.

That spring we were flooded out. The cabin sat on low
ground, so when all the snow melted and Clarke's Brook behind
the meadow overtopped its banks, it was only a few nights before
the water stole under our door. I woke to the sound of splash-
ing, and was carried in high glee from my bunk. At daylight that
March morning, we beat a retreat to the summer house, prefer-
ring drafts to drowning. I didn't go back that year, except to enjoy
the odd sensation of skating in my bedroom.

And that was life for a boy in a winter house. Many of my
playmates lived the same way. Not all summer houses were as
drafty as ours, of course; custom played some part in this hiber-
nal living. Certainly economy didn't, for the only actual saving
was in fuel wood—which was abundant anyway. Outright poverty explained the pattern with some, for they lived in their log
houses winter and summer. But a winter house is no good for
summer living. Their children missed a lot.

No, it was not poverty. Rather, it was a peculiar affluence
our forebears bequeathed us when they abandoned their sea-
pounded fishing hamlets for sheltered, wooded inlets like our bay.

Their comrades who stayed to ply oar and jigger pinned on them the derisive label of "baymen." But the plenitude of fresh meat, garden space, and wood soon salved the sting away. Soon, in fact, as they sat in their snug cabins and chatted of harder times, they came to adopt "outsiders" as the name for their seafaring neighbours and "the outside" as the place where they lived.

The winter house thus occupied a transition zone between that century and this. Sitting now within earshot of passing cars in this modern house, I feel gratitude that my generation was able to inherit, while yet children, some of that pioneering tradition.

I can see it now—a Christmas-card cottage come to life; tree-sheltered, snow-mantled, bright-windowed, in a lilac dusk.

My Christmas Concert
Wayne Curtis

When I was a schoolboy, the teachers were local women who, not having gone to teachers' college, taught on local licences. It was a common thing in the 1920s, especially in a one-room elementary school like the one I attended.

For years I sat in a classroom where my sister Lillian (who *had* graduated from Normal School in 1914), was in charge. She told me to stand by my desk and read from the first and second primers (learning guides), then sing along with her the old school songs—"The Maple Leaf Forever" and "O Canada." I got bored, and gave it up to help my father in the woods.

When I was in my late teens, our school was going to close because of poor attendance. They needed one more pupil before a teacher could be hired, so Papa sent me back to the classroom. The teacher, a Miss Bernice Underhill, agreed to come from Blackville. She would pay room and board at our home. Each morning I walked with her to the school, where I was in charge of keeping the fire going. I also shovelled the doorsteps, as well as a pathway to the outhouses and the woodshed. Plus, I carried drinking water from the home of Clark Keenan, which was just across the field.

With these jobs done, I spent my time drawing potatoes on a slate, or listening to the little ones attempting to spell "mother." I was a grown man sitting among children and embarrassed to be there. But Papa needed the board money, and some education was essential for the smaller ones. I had three sisters in school. Still, there were times when that little three-windowed, clapboard building was closed for months, even years.

There was a rag-barrel smell in that old school—the damp coats that hung from nails in the wainscotting; the broken chalk that lay on ledges of blackboard; the musty, cloth-bound readers (*Up and Away, All Sails Set, Life and Adventure*) slanting down the shelf, the Mountie and totem pole images on their covers fading with the afternoon light. I sat near the door and listened to freedom: blue jays crying in hawthorn trees, crickets in the playground, a wind that rattled the ropes on our flagstaff. Those breezes carried the smell of decaying leaves, the perfume of distant bonfires, and, in early December, the dampness of new snow.

I glanced out a window to see winter coming, wishing I were in the woods where I could earn a few dollars. Even now, these reflections repeat inside me, each from a different state of mind, a different need. They live on in those old school smells and songs, like coals in the ash of burnt-out fantasies.

As the season advanced, everything was influenced by the quickly approaching yuletide. Behind our house, the woods had suddenly become scattered with little red berries and pine buds, the trees taking on new shades of silver, a stronger scent of balsam. Snow clung to boughs, leaving bare patches of moss that crunched under my feet. Deer tracks froze into heart-shaped impressions, and our window glass became a frosted wonderland.

Even the old school had grasped the spirit. The redundant carol singing and recitations were proof of it.

In class, Miss Underhill was strict. We were not allowed to whisper. She'd sit with a sweater over her shoulders, her feet upon the stove's damper.

"John, go to the shed and fetch more firewood," she would say. "This place is cold as a barn."

"Yes, Teacher," I'd reply.

It was great to get outside, if only for a few minutes. Once I spilled an armload of split maple, pretending to trip and fall as I came in through the door. Chunks scattered into the aisles. There was laughter. I did this not to provoke the teacher, but more as a respite against a relentless afternoon. But it was not funny. As I gathered the sticks, I realized it.

During dinner hour, the teacher, at the doorstep, gazed through a cloud of powdered chalk as she clapped two red, white, and blue erasers together. If we were not in sight, she gave the bell an angry shake. And we ran to line up before her—the girls in front, the bigger boys in the back—to march in and wait for her words, "Please be seated."

By mid-December, we were in the final stages of rehearsal for the Christmas concert—recitations, songs, and dialogues. With coloured chalk, the girls had painted little holly leaves and berries along the edges of the blackboard. Crayoned drawings were pasted to windows. I was asked to scrub the floor. The classroom smelled of Creolin and new stove polish. Later I was sent to the woods for a Christmas tree, which we decorated with hawthorn and rose hip, plus strings of frozen cranberries. Under it, we placed our gifts for the teacher.

On examination day, I carried in chairs from around the community, filling the aisles and the back of the classroom. The school was filled with magic. After lunch, it was snowing softly as we sat and waited for parents to arrive. Miss Underhill paced the floor, her delicate fingers playing with her beads as though in prayer. She stopped only to look out the window, past the crayoned Santas to the stretch of road that led up the hill to our school. It was like the day was hurrying past, to defy us all.

No one was coming to the concert. At two forty-five, she decided to go ahead with the program.

There were giggles as I embarrassingly gave my recitation in front of a dozen empty chairs and the class, who had heard it a hundred times.

> *Away up in the rocky north,*
> *Where Christmas trees won't grow,*
> *All snug and cozy in his bed*
> *Lives a little Eskimo.*
> *His tiny stockings and mukluks*
> *He hangs up by the fire,*
> *He lives so close to Santa Claus,*
> *The reindeer never tire.*

I took a bow and sat down. There was applause—not for me, but more for the liberty of making a noise, here. The five schoolgirls of the community, my sisters among them, stood across the front of the room and sang:

> *Santa Claus is coming,*
> *We will welcome him with glee,*
> *We'll hang a gift for everyone upon our Christmas tree…*
> *Hurrah, hurrah.*

And with each "hurrah," their hands made a sweeping gesture, as if to grab something invisible from the air. They bowed and went to their seats.

I went outside, stood in the entry, and on queue, came in as a beggar man looking for a remedy for his aching back. I rolled on the floor, moaned and gasped from pain, exaggerating the scene to try and create a bit of excitement. The children broke into pockets of laughter. Even our teacher, who had no time for folly, offered a sad half-smile.

After the program, as I prepared to return the chairs to the neighbours' houses, Miss Underhill, sitting at her desk, took a handkerchief from her sleeve. She wiped her nose and dabbed her eyes. "Christmastime," she sobbed, "I thought some of the parents just might come."

The next day, snow slid off roofs and drifted into dooryards to make cliffs in the lee of buildings. Flowerpots on verandas became tubs of ice cream. Fence posts became Popsicles, and in the field, the shaggy spruce grew into giant bells as I gathered the dead limbs of apple trees for the hearth fire.

For the little ones, my father made a big ado about Santa keeping his suit clean against the black ash of our chimney. I remember the children's restless night that followed, the turkey, the church service, the visits from neighbours.

But then suddenly, amid all the singing, the fear of a storm, and the hearth fires, as though the whole scene had been executed by a magician, Christmas had come and gone without us even seeing it happen. It was like reality had gobbled up our pre-Christmas illusions. Everything we had looked forward to for months was over in hours. The cap guns and the plastic-faced dolls with their tilting blue eyes, the fire engines and the twisted candy canes, lay scattered in a haze of falsified hopes and selfish dreams. And, disillusioned with ourselves and each other, we were left trying to adjust back into the harsh old world of winter.

Like the school concert, the joy of Christmas had been in the preparations.

From *The Sailing Spirit*
John Hughes

O n the evening of December 23, at 1920 hours, *Joseph Young* and I sailed quietly past Cabo Island Lighthouse in a gentle southwesterly breeze to begin the last 260-mile stretch up the coast to Sydney. The gale-force, or near-gale-force, winds that had been with us for so many days now had finally abated. Through the binoculars, I stared at the rocky promontory upon which the light had been built. It was here, in the first BOC Challenge in 1982, that the race had ended for one of the competitors. Exhausted, he had overslept and been driven on to the rocks by the current and a shifting wind. A chill crept over me at the thought. I vowed not to crawl into my bunk before *Joseph Young* was safely tied to the dock. The fact that I hadn't closed my eyes for nearly three days made me that much more afraid. In my present state, I knew that once I fell asleep, no alarm clock on earth would be able to rouse me. With luck, I would reach Sydney in another thirty-six hours. I simply had to hang on and hope for a fair wind.

Sitting up on the cockpit coaming, leaning back against the lifelines, I watched the lights of towns and villages, less than a mile off on the port side, slip by in the darkness. It was becoming a struggle to stay awake, and I found my mind wandering. With a jerk, I sat bolt upright, the hair on the nape of my neck rising—I had heard the unmistakable sound of someone exhaling loudly right behind me! Spinning around, eyes wide, I peered over the rail. Under the water, I saw a movement, and jumped back with a start as a large dolphin broke the surface and blew. Feeling a little foolish, I watched as half a dozen of the creatures gradually appeared, and swam alongside for a while. As always, I was captivated by their beauty and was sorry when they finally vanished from sight.

When the sun came up in the morning, it brought with it a change of climate that was almost unbelievable. On the chat hour, the competitors who had gone before had all remarked how it seemed, when they rounded Gabo Island, that they had passed into a completely different world. Gone were the grey skies, the monstrous swells, the persistent cold, and the wicked gales. It was like being transported from the Arctic Ocean to the tropics in the blink of an eye. The water now was a beautiful blue, the sun beat down from a clear sky, and the temperature soared. Peeling off foul-weather gear and layers of thermal underwear, I dug out shorts, sneakers, and a T-shirt. The rigging was soon festooned with sodden bedding, and woollen clothing of every description. Sailing close inshore to avoid the south-setting current farther out, I marvelled at the fantastic beaches and the thick vegetation. It was hard to believe that this was Christmas Eve, a time, in my experience, for snow and cold!

As the afternoon came on, the second wind that I had felt at dawn faded, and exhaustion began to overtake me. Despite the fact that the open ocean stretched out for hundreds of miles on my starboard side, I couldn't shake the feeling that I was sailing up a channel. I kept returning to the table to pore over the chart, finding it more and more difficult to orientate myself with respect to the land. My eyes felt as if they were full of sand, and the glaring sun and heat, which had been so welcome in the morning, were now taking their toll. I knew that what I desperately needed was sleep, but the more tired I became, the greater was my fear of not waking until it was too late. I was convinced that disaster lurked just around the corner, waiting for me to lie down. It was a bizarre sensation.

Christmas Eve, almost midnight. My last night at sea for a while, I hoped. Tuned to a local FM radio station, I listened to Christmas carols. Even they could do little to raise my spirits. The wind had dropped since dusk, and although I was only sixty miles from the finish line, at this speed it would be twenty hours before I could drop the sails for the last time. It looked like my goal of finishing this leg in under forty days was slipping out of reach.

At one o'clock in the morning, December 25, I wrote in the logbook the first entry for the day. It read, "Becalmed. Great. Merry Christmas." Thoroughly dejected, I crawled back on deck to keep a lookout and wait for even the slightest breeze. The thought of having to endure another day of this was almost too much to bear. What happened next remains a bit of a mystery to me.

I came to with a start. I was perched on the starboard lifelines—stark naked! I had fallen asleep, my head on my knees, having removed my safety harness and clothes somewhere along the way. Badly shaken, I hurried below to put on a pot of coffee and bring myself to my senses. I looked at the time and saw that several hours had passed without my knowing. Cautiously, I crept back on deck for a look around. Off to the east, the sun was still below the horizon, but the night was rapidly giving way to dawn. To the west, land was barely visible a few miles away. I had given myself a hell of a fright with this turn of events, and, gathering up harness and clothes from the cockpit, I realized how lucky I had been. Tripping on something, I stared in amazement; my flashlight was jammed down in the drain. It took a good tug to pull it free. What on earth had I been doing? Retreating below, I poured a cup of coffee and put my clothes back on. This sort of behaviour just wouldn't do!

By 0800 hours, we were moving slowly northward again under the influence of a light southerly wind. I had the large number one genoa poled out to port, nicely balancing the mainsail. We were back in close to the shore, and with only forty miles to go, I prayed that the wind would pick up a little and stay out of the south. Promptly at 0900 hours, I picked up the VHF radio and placed a call to race headquarters in Sydney. It was a real relief to hear a friendly voice, and to receive a few words of encouragement. When pressed for an estimated time of arrival, however, the best I could do was tell them where I was and what the wind was like at present. While I was talking, a sudden loud flap from the sails sent a shudder through the boat. Quickly terminating the call, I hurried on deck to see what was going on. To my surprise, *Joseph Young* was now sailing backwards. The wind had shifted instantly through 180 degrees and was now blowing from dead ahead. With the boom held out by a preventer, and the spinnaker pole rigged for the headsail, we were going astern at about three knots! This was potentially dangerous. It seemed to take ages to get the boat sorted out and heading off on the port tack with the sails trimmed properly. I was well aware that I was reacting like a punch-drunk boxer. I was beyond tiredness, and stayed on my hands and knees as I moved about the deck. The breeze had increased slightly with the change in direction, which was the good news, the bad news being that I would now have to tack back and forth all the way to Sydney.

Two hours later, I was crouched on the bow of the boat, sobbing with frustration and fatigue as I struggled to change the number one for the number three jib. The wind was increasing rapidly, and I felt that life was just bloody unfair. This was turning into a repeat of my arrival in Cape Town, where I had had to beat straight into a gale to reach port.

By evening, *Joseph Young* was punching into a rough sea, and I knew that I would be crossing the finish line in darkness. Ahead, I could see the cliffs that marked the entrance to Sydney Harbour, but it was very nearly 2300 hours before I had worked my way that far north. By then, of course, I was in contact with Robin Knox-Johnston on board the committee boat at the finish. I was also very confused, due largely to being utterly exhausted. To enter the harbour and reach the finish line, I first had to pass through a wide break in the cliffs known as Sydney Heads. The chart showed a flashing light on either side of this gap. From the deck of *Joseph Young*, a mile offshore, I could pick out only the light marking the southern Head. Knowing that my judgment was impaired by fatigue, and dazzled by the lights of the city in the background, I was terrified of making a mistake. Over the radio, I told Robin of my fears and said that I refused to head in for the land without being absolutely certain that I was where I thought I was. Visions of *Joseph Young* being smashed to pieces on the rocks ran through my mind. I suggested that perhaps I would head offshore, and return in daylight. For what happened next, I will be forever in Robin's debt. Telling me to hang on, he brought the committee boat out between the cliffs. Once in position, he pointed his searchlight to the east and flashed an agreed-upon signal. From out to sea, I gave a shout of relief as I saw the wink of his light beckoning me in to safety. Grabbing the radio mike, I let him know I was on my way.

Ten minutes later, I was racing in past the harbour entrance, flanked by the committee boat and a police launch. Blinded by their lights, disorientated by the noise and activity, the first indication I had of having crossed the finish line was the wail of their sirens. Thankfully, I luffed into the wind and rushed forward to douse the jib. Unfortunately, however, the self-steering had developed a small fault less than an hour before, and now, with the helm unattended, we began to bear off, which allowed the wind to catch the mainsail. Hurriedly stowing the jib, I dashed back aft, shouting a warning to the police launch, which now lay directly in front of a rapidly accelerating *Joseph Young*. Except for their quick action, I would have had the distinction of being the first BOC yacht to ram the welcoming police boat!

Disaster momentarily averted, I dropped the mainsail and gratefully caught the tow line tossed over from the launch. The second leg of the race was over. The time was ten minutes to midnight, Christmas Day; thirty-nine days, twenty-three hours, and fifty minutes since the starting gun had been fired in Cape Town. By the skin of my teeth, I had made it within my target of forty days.

New Brunswick's First Santa Claus
David Goss

When Charles A. Sampson died in his ninetieth year on November 15, 1929, the *Fredericton Gleaner* described him in a bold back-page headline as a "grand old man." Above his photo, only slightly smaller print stated he had been "40 years secretary of the School Board Trustees, Secretary of the Victoria Hospital Board, Past Grand Master of the Odd Fellows, and a lifelong member and officer of the Methodist (Wilmot) Church."

Further, it noted he had been "beloved by all that knew him." But the article made no mention of those who knew him as Santa Claus...or that he was indeed the first Santa that New Brunswick children ever visited, or received gifts from.

Sampson was born in St. Andrews in 1840, and studied at the Baptist seminary in Fredericton. His first job was as a printer with the *Royal Gazette*. His love for the outdoors led him to the express business, then conducted by stagecoach and steamboat. He served upriver as far as the Woodstock area, and made trips by sea from Saint John to Boston. When he froze his hands on one of the upriver trips (having given up his seat to a dignitary, to ride outside with the stage driver), he decided to open a confectionery shop opposite the Officers' Barracks on Queen Street in 1867. He brought in a French confectioner from Boston to get him established.

In the *Colonial Farmer* of December 21, 1867, Sampson ran a surprising advertisement: "1867 Xmas 1868. Santa Claus has appointed Charles A Sampson, Confectioner, agent for the sale of all sorts of Fancy Confectionery for the Holiday Season," and thereafter followed a list of all his products for sale.

Perhaps Sampson or his new confectioner from Boston had heard of the J. W. Parkinson store in Philadelphia, advertised as Kriss Kringle's headquarters. According to Gerry Bowler's *World Encyclopedia of Christmas*, Parkinson's was the only store on the east coast to have a "real Cris Cringle" appear until 1890, when Boston had the second. It seems Bowler overlooked Sampson of Fredericton. I'll tell you why.

In 1867, only one other Fredericton merchant, James L. Beverly, seller of books, stationery, and toys, mentions Santa. In 1868, Felix Protous, at Queen and Westmorland streets, billed himself as the Santa Claus Depot and sold candy, toys, and bonbons. The following year, Sampson moves ahead of the competition with an advertisement dated December 4:

> *Co-partnership notice:*
>
> Santa Claus and Sampson's have this day entered into a co-partnership in order more fully to meet the demands of parents as well as their children during the coming holiday season.
>
> The new firm proposes an arrangement entirely new and novel in this part of the province, but extensively practised elsewhere, and found to be a great saving of trouble to parents.

Parties residing in the city can bring their children's socks to our Establishment Thursday or Friday the 23rd and 24th inst., and OLD SANTA will carefully fill them with the choicest Confectionery, Nuts, · *Fruit, Toys, etc....*

Later that year, Sampson solidified his position by noting that the "co-partnership entered into between Sampson and Santa had been ratified by the Dominion government."

His efforts seem to have paid off, for in January 1870, he advertised that he had "added new machinery to his establishment." At year end, he noted his expanded service to areas outside the city such as Bright, Keswick, Bristol, Oromocto, and Sheffield.

We have no record of Christmas 1871 because both papers, the *New Brunswick Reporter* and the *Colonial Farmer*, have issues missing for the Christmas period. But the tone of his 1872 advertisement indicates that, on December 24 of that year, Sampson moved out of his shop and into the community in the role of Santa.

In the *Colonial Farmer* of December 23, his advertisement read: "The attention of the public is directed to an entirely new and novel arrangement the undersigned has made this year in order to aid...the time-honoured custom of Santa Claus' visit on Christmas Eve," He went on to explain that all goods purchased at his shop would be delivered by Santa Claus himself on Christmas Eve.

"He will make his entry into Fredericton some time on Monday night 22nd inst, probably about nine o'clock, and will drive through the principal streets for a short time to take a view of the chimneys in houses of those who do not wish him to call at the door." And on December 24, Sampson did just that. The next day, Christmas, Fredericton children were invited to Sampson's shop for a small gift.

On December 23, 1873, the *Colonial Farmer* noted that "Charles Sampson, shopkeeper, shows one of the most brilliant and tempting assortment of Holiday presents...his Santa Claus is a novel innovation who delivers on Christmas eve."

In 1874, Sampson advertised his "third visible appearance" of Santa, and encouraged the parents of Gibson and St. Mary's to let their children "remain up to see him arrive." He stated that he would "deliver stockings left at Sampson's," and "goods purchased at any of the stores in town...for ten cents per package."

That year, too, he provided a photo taken by Fredericton photographer Tuck, and engraved in New York so the *New Brunswick Reporter* could run it to alleviate any lingering fears that Santa might prove frightening to area children. Though he advertised on December 15, 1875, that "final particulars on the arrival of Santa Claus will be furnished to the children next week," on December 22 he placed a further advertisement noting it would "not be possible for Santa Claus to arrive this year." However, he would have a "large Christmas tree in his store," and "every good boy and girl in town will receive a Christmas box on...Christmas morning. However, any boy applying twice will get no candy during the winter."

A later report noted more than five hundred children benefited from his generosity, and no doubt some were among those who agreed with the *Gleaner*'s note on his death that he had been a "grand old man."

Angel Wings
Dorothy Winslow Wright

I raced down the warm, steamy school hallway buttoning my coat, pushed the door open, and stepped into the icy December blast. I was late, and hoped Josie was still waiting for me. I had news for her. I was going to be in the Christmas play. An angel! Not only that, I was the only eighth grader to be chosen. The rest of the cast were ninth graders, but Mrs. Smythe wanted someone my size and colouring to be the front angel. Maybe my curly red hair wasn't so bad after all.

Josie was gone, but I wasn't too upset. I had things to think about, and I didn't have time to go to her house anyway. I needed to hunt up two wire coat hangers and some tissue paper to make my wings. I gave the sheet of directions a quick glance and stuffed it in my pocket. I'd seen wings like those before. They were easy to make.

"Don't bother with the tinsel," Mrs. Smythe had said. "We'll trim the wings at school when we make your halo."

Mum was still at work when I reached the apartment. I let myself in, tossed my books on a chair, and rummaged through the closet. I found the coat hangers, but the tissue paper was too wrinkled to use. I would have to buy some and I wasn't sure how that would strike my mother. Since the divorce, money was tight.

I needn't have worried. As soon as I told her, Mum took over. When I showed her the directions, she scoffed. "If you're going to be an angel," she said, "we'll make you proper wings, not something flimsy like that."

Suddenly I was uneasy. Mum had a way of overdoing things when her enthusiasm was up. I learned that in my fifth-grade sewing class. She bought the best quality green plaid cotton she could find, not the small, random print specified. "If you're going to make a dress," Mum had said, "you might as well have something that will go with your pretty red hair."

The sewing teacher had not been pleased. Every time we worked on our dresses, she sputtered about having to take time to match the plaid. She was more particular about my work than that of the other students, making me rip out seams again and again. "They must be perfect," she said, "to suit so fancy a dress."

Mrs. Smythe was a different sort of teacher. Her bearing was starchy New England, yet wisps of lavender grey springing from her pompadour softened her stiffness. On cold days she wore a lacy, rose-coloured sweater over her prim white blouse. It brought out the pink in her cheeks. Made her almost pretty. I admired Mrs. Smythe and I didn't want anything to disrupt the rapport between us.

But there was no stopping Mum. "Oh, Dossie," she bubbled, when she came in the next night, "wait till you see the wings we'll make! Look at this!" She handed me a roll of wire and a package of white crepe paper—the wrong kind of paper.

"Crepe paper is easier to work with than tissue paper," she explained later that evening, "and it is certainly more sturdy. Now, stand up and turn your back to me while I shape the wire."

Within minutes, she had designed the most perfect pair of wings. Full, rounded tops tapered to graceful curves. The stretched paper, glued in place, was taut. Shimmery. She wired the wings together, then added the white elastic that would hold the wings in place.

I modelled them for her. "They're coming along," she said, "but they still need feathers."

"They don't need any feathers, Mum—really," I protested. "They're perfect the way they are." As the wings were then, I didn't think Mrs. Smythe would object too much. But feathers—I didn't know how she'd react to that.

"Don't worry, Dossie, I know how to make angel wings," Mum said, misunderstanding my doubts. "And I want to do this for you. I feel badly enough that your play is scheduled when I'm at work. The least I can do is help you in the costume department. And you're going to be one beautiful angel, sweetie—just you wait and see."

She cut the remaining crepe paper into fat strips, then slashed, trimmed, and snipped the edges. When she unfolded the first strip and began to wind the fringe around the wing, the wing took on a life of its own. Mum was right. That was the wing of a real angel.

The next morning, I carried the finished wings to school—a long, awkward, finger-numbing walk. But it was worth it. When Mrs. Smythe saw them, she beamed. "What beautiful wings," she said. "Wherever did you get them?"

"My mother made them...last night."

"She did. Well, she is very creative..."

Along with her compliments, Mrs. Smythe managed to get the message across to me that I would be doing the school a real service if I let Glenda, a tall ninth grader with a speaking part, wear my wings. "...it wouldn't be appropriate for the smallest angel to have the biggest wings, now would it."

I stared at the floor. Did Mrs. Smythe think I was trying to make myself better than the other angels? It was all I could do to hold back the tears.

"I'll take care of making your wings, Dorothy," Mrs. Smythe said, her voice warmer than usual. "I know your mother worked hard on these and she shouldn't have to make another pair."

Telling Mum would be the problem. How could I ever make her understand? Not only that, she'd invested money she didn't have.

I walked home with Josie, keeping silent about the wings. She hadn't seen them. She didn't know what had gone on, and I didn't feel like telling her.

"You act mad," Josie said. "Are you mad at me for not waiting the other day?"

"No, I was late. I just wish I wasn't in the Christmas play. All the kids are older than I am. It's no fun."

"Why don't you drop out?"

"Mum would never understand."

"Yeah, but if she's gotta work, how'd she know if you were in it or not?"

I didn't answer. When I left Josie at the corner, I went into the dark apartment alone. I flopped in the chair by the window and watched the snow flurries skitter down the street. What would I do? I still hadn't decided when I heard Mum unlock the door.

"Why is it so dark in here?" she asked. She snapped on the lamp, then plugged in the lights of our tiny tabletop Christmas tree. She walked over to me and peered in my face. "Hmm," she said, "things can't be *that* bad. What's wrong? Did you drop your wings in the snow?"

"No, nothing like that."

"Well, that's good. How did Mrs. Smythe like them? Bet she thought they were really something."

"She did. She loved 'em."

"Then what are you upset about, sweetie? It's Christmas. We have our tree, and you're going to be an angel in the school play. What are you singing, anyway?"

"'Angels We Have Heard On High.' That's all. Mostly we just stand around and listen to the others."

"Glo-o-o-ria," Mum crooned as she slipped out of her worn black coat. She shook off the snow and hung it up. She looked tired in spite of her singing. Singing for my benefit. Singing to cheer me up.

I knew right then I could not back out of the play. I also knew I couldn't tell her that someone else was going to wear my angel wings.

Two weeks later, I stood at the stage entrance with the rest of the white-robed angels. A silver halo skimmed my hair. A pair of tissue-paper wings lay lightly on my shoulders.

"You look beautiful, Dorothy," Mrs. Smythe whispered, "and thank you for letting Glenda wear your wings."

"Lo, I bring you tidings of great joy..." Glenda began.

Soon we were tiptoeing in. The spotlight struck the fringe of Glenda's wings. They rustled in the light breeze as if alive, as if Glenda truly was the angel of God. When we sang "Gloria in excelsis Deo," I meant every word of it. I was no longer on the wooden stage of a junior high school, I was in Bethlehem, announcing to the world the joy of Christmas.

When the play was over and school was out, I carried my wings home and stood them in the corner of the living room. They were the first thing Mum saw when she came in that night.

"How did everything go?" she asked.

"Perfect. Nobody made any mistakes."

"...and the wings?"

"They were the best ones in the whole play."

"I wish I could have been there, but I know you were a beautiful angel."

"That's what Mrs. Smythe said." I grinned.

"So it was worth the effort to make those wings, wasn't it?"

I nodded. Everything was as it should be. Mum's wings had made the play better. What difference did it make who wore them? I hadn't seen Mum look that happy in a long time.

From *Bread and Molasses*
Andy MacDonald

It seemed that we didn't get enough to eat even on Christmas Day. One Christmas morning, Murray and I got an orange cardboard duck each from Santa. They had picked up a beautiful Christmas smell from the oranges in the bottoms of our socks. Taking our ducks with us out to the old, vacant henhouse, we smelled them every step of the way. We were determined that if the smell continued, there was nothing else to do but eat them and satisfy the craving for the smell that almost drove us wild.

Murray went at his first, starting from the head. Then I decapitated mine, and it took us twenty minutes before our toy cardboard ducks were devoured, with us savouring every morsel. It took a lot of saliva to chew up this pasteboard, but that didn't bother us, as that beautiful smell lingered on even when the ducks were in our stomachs.

Now that everything edible was gone, all we had to look forward to was the same boring routine of school again.

What a letdown it was to come back to school—books and pencils in the same positions you had left them before Christmas. Teachers had a different attitude toward life. Last time they were bubbling with love. Now it was the "well, we've wasted a lot of time" kind of Scrooge attitude. I thought this wasn't right, and began planning my hooky. If only the teacher had sighed after Christmas and said, "Well, darn, we have six months of school left, and I hate it as much as you." Then I might have stuck it out. But she let us know in no uncertain terms she was going to be tough—no more time to waste. I was wondering why I should put in another day of this outright nonsense.

Why should I care if sisal hemp came from the town of Sisal? I could do without sisal. Who needed wool from Argentina? All Pa had to do was go to the store and there was wool right there. Ninety-eight cents for a sweater, which if caught in the rain would require a major operation to remove.

This terrible letdown after Christmas and New Year's still haunts me today. Excitement, love, and everything that goes with it would come to a very abrupt halt.

Our tree was never taken down until nearly the middle of January, its spruce needles quite thin after being in a hot room since December 1. Ten-year-old strung popcorn would be taken off the tree and put away for the next Christmas. During hungry spells, we'd sneak up to the attic and eat the aged popcorn.

How Santa Claus Came to Cape St. Anthony
Wilfred T. Grenfell

A universal robe of white had long covered our countryside, hiding every vestige of our rocky soil, and every trace of the great summer fishery. The mail steamer had paid its last visit for six months; and thus the last link with civilization was broken. Even the loitering sea ducks and lesser auks had left us. The iron grip of winter lay on sea and shore.

At its best, the land here scarcely suggests the word "country" to a southerner—even the word "moors." For the rock is everywhere close to the surface, and mosses and lichens are its chief products. The larger part of the country we call barrens. Few of the houses deserve even to be called cottages, for all are of light, rough wood. Most are of only one story and contain but two rooms. The word "huts" would convey a more accurate idea of these humble abodes. The settlements themselves are small and scattered, and at this time the empty tilts of the summer fishermen give a still more desolate aspect to these lonely habitations.

Early in December, we had been dumped from the little mail steamer on the harbour ice about half a mile from shore, and hauled up to the little mission hospital where we were to make our headquarters for the winter. The name of our harbour was St. Anthony. Christmas was close upon us. The prospect of enjoying the conventional pleasures of the season was not bright. Not unnaturally, our thoughts went over the sea to the family gathering at home, at which our places would be vacant. We should miss the holly and mistletoe, the roast beef and plum pudding, the inevitable crackers, and the giving and receiving of presents, which had always seemed essential to a full enjoyment of the Christmas holiday.

We soon found that few of the children here had ever possessed a toy, and that there was scarcely a single girl who owned a doll. Now and again one would see, nailed high up on the wall, well out of reach of the children, a flimsy, cheaply painted doll; and the mother would explain that her "pa had got un from a trader, sir, for thirty cents. No, us don't allow Nellie to have it, 'feared lest she might spoil un"— a fear I found to be only too well grounded when I came to examine its anatomy more closely.

Christmas trees in plenty grew near the hospital; and we could easily arrange for a Father Christmas. The only question was whether our stock of toys would justify us in inviting so many children as would want to come. It is easy to satisfy children like these, however, and so we announced that we expected Santa Claus on a certain day. There was great talk about the affair. Whispers reached us that Aunt Mary thought her "Joe weren't too big to come; sure, he'd be only sixteen." May White was only going eighteen, and she would so like to come. Old Daddy Gilliam would like to sit in a corner. He'd never seen a Christmas tree, and he was nigh on eighty. We were obliged to yield, and with guilty consciences expected twice as many as the room would hold. All through the day before the event, the Sister was busy making buns; and it was even whispered that a barrel of apples had been carried over to the room.

In the evening, a sick call carried me north to a tiny place on the Strait of Belle Isle, where a woman lay in great pain, and by all accounts dying. The dogs were in great form, and travelling was fair enough till we came to a great arm of the sea, which lay right in our path and was only recently caught over with young ice. To reach the other shore, we had to make a wide detour, bumping our way along the rough edge of the old standing ice. Even here, the salt water came up through the snow, and the dogs sank to their shoulders in a cold mush that made each mile into a half-dozen. We began to think that our chance of getting back in time on the morrow was small indeed. We were also wondering that it seemed to be a real disappointment to ourselves that we should miss the humble attempt at Christmas keeping.

One thing went a long way toward reconciling us to the disappointment. The case we had come to see proved to be one in which skilled help was of real service. So we were a contented company round the log fire in the little hut as we sat listening to stories from one and another of the neighbours, who, according to custom, had dropped in to see the stranger. Before long, my sleeping bag was loudly calling to me, after the exercise of the day. "We must be off by dawn, Uncle Phil, for there's no counting on these short days, and we have promised to see that Santa Claus is in time for the Christmas tree tomorrow night at St. Anthony." Soon, stretched out on the floor, we slept as soundly as in a featherbed.

Only a few minutes seemed to have passed when, "'Twill be dawning shortly, Doctor," in the familiar tones of my driver's voice, came filtering into my bag. "Right you are, Rube; put the kettle on and call the dogs; I will be ready in a couple of shakes."

Oh, what a glorious morning! An absolute stillness, and the air as sweet as sugar. Everywhere a mantle of perfect white below, a fathomless depth of cloudless blue overhead— and the first radiance of the coming day blending one into the other with a rich, transparent red. The bracing cold made one feel twenty years younger. We found it a hard job to tackle up the dogs, they were so mad to be off. As we topped the first hill, the great bay that had caused us so much trouble lay below us, and my driver gave a joyous shout. "Hurrah, Doctor! There's a lead for us." Far out on the ice, he had spied a black speck moving toward the opposite shore. A komatik had ventured over the young ice, and to follow it would mean a saving of five miles to us.

We had made a good landing and scaled the opposite hill, and were galloping over the high barrens, when the dogs began to give tongue, loudly announcing that a team was coming from the opposite direction. As we drew near, a muffled figure jumped off, and hauling his dogs to one side, shouted the customary, "What cheer?"

Then a surprised, "The doctor, as I live! You're the very man I'm after. Why, there's komatiks gone all over the country after you. A lad has shot hisself down at St. Ronald's, and he's bleeding shocking."

"All right, Jake, old friend. The turn for the path is off the big pond, is it not?"

"That's it, Doctor, but I'm coming along anyhow, 'feared I might be wanted."

My little leader must have overheard this conversation, for she simply flew over the hills. Yet it was already dusk when at length we shot down the semi-precipice, on the side of which the little house clings like a barnacle. The anxious crowd, gathered to await our arrival, disappeared before the avalanche like a morning mist when the sun rises. Following direction, I found myself in a tiny, naked room, already filled with well-meaning visitors, though they were able to do nothing but look on and defile what little air made its way in through the fixed windows. Fortunately, for want of putty, air leaked in around the glass.

Stretched on the floor behind the stove lay a pale-faced boy of about ten years. His clothes had been taken off, and an old patchwork quilt covered his body. His right thigh was covered with a heterogeneous mass of bloody rags. Sitting by him was his mother, her forehead resting in her hands as if she were wrestling with some inscrutable problem. She rose as I entered with: "Tis Clem, Doctor. He got Dick here to give him the gun to try and shoot a gull, and there were a high ballicater of ice in the way, and he were trying to climb up over it, and she went off and shot him, and us doesn't know what to do next—next, and—"

While she ran on with her story, I cleared the room of visitors, and kneeling down by the boy, removed the dirty mass of rags that had been used to stanch the blood. The charge had entered the thigh at close quarters above the knee, and passed downward, blowing the kneecap to pieces. Most of it had passed out again. The loose fragments of bone still adhering to the ragged flesh, the fragments of clothing blown into it, and the foul smell and discolouration added by the gunpowder made the outlook a very ugly one. Moreover, there rose to my mind the memory of a similar case in which we had come too late, blood poisoning having set in, and the child having died after much suffering.

The mother had by this time quieted down, and was simply repeating, "What shall us do?"

"There's only one thing to be done. We must pack Clem up and carry him to the hospital right away."

"Iss, Doctor, that's the only way, I'm thinking," she replied. "An' I suppose you'll cut off his leg, and he'll never walk no more, and oh, dear! What—"

"Come, tear up this calico into strips and bring me some boiling water—mind, it must be well boiled; and get me that board over there—'twill serve to make a splint; and then go and tell Dick to get the dogs ready at once; for we've a Christmas tree at St. Anthony tonight, and I must be back at all costs."

In this way we kept her too busy to worry or hesitate about letting the child go; for we well knew it was his only chance, and she had never seen a hospital, and the idea of one was as terrifying as a morgue.

"Home, home, home!" to the dogs—and once again our steel runners are humming over the crisp snow. Now in the darkness we are clinging tightly to our hand ropes as we shoot over the hills. Now the hospital lights are coming up, and now the lights in the windows of the room. As we get near, they look so numerous and so cheerful that we seem to be approaching a town. Now we can hear the merry ring of the children's voices, and can make out a crowd of figures gathered around the doorway. They are waiting for the tardy arrival of "Sandy Claws." Of course, we are at once recognized, and there is a general hush of disappointment, as if they had thought at last "Sandy" himself was come.

"He is only a little way behind us," we shouted. "He is coming like a whirlwind. Look out, everybody, when he gets here. Don't get too close to his dogs."

Only a little while later, and the barking of dogs announces the approach of the other komatik. But we alone are in the secret of its real mission. Someone is calling from the darkness, and a long sleigh with a double-banked team of dogs has drawn up opposite the doorway. Two fur-clad figures standing by it steady a huge box that is lashed upon it. The light shining on the near one reveals of his muffled face only two sparkling eyes and large icicles bristling over the muffler from heavy mustache and whiskers, like the ivory tusks of some old bull walrus. Both figures are panting with exertion, and blowing out great clouds of steam like galloping horses on a frosty morning. There could be no doubt about it this time. Here was the real "Sandy Claws" at last, come mysteriously over the snow with his dogs and komatik and big box and all!

The excitement of the crowd, already intense from anxiety over our own delay, now knew no bounds. Where had they come from? What could be in that big box? How large it looked in the darkness! Could it have really been dragged all the way from the North Pole? Luckily, no one had the courage left to go near enough to discover the truth.

The hospital door was swung open, and a loud voice cried out: "Welcome, welcome, 'Sandy Claws!' We're all so glad you've come; we thought you'd forgotten us. Come right in. Come right in! Oh, no! don't think of undoing the box outside; why, you'll freeze all those toys out there! Just unlash it and bring it right in as it is. Come in; there's a cup of tea waiting for you before you go over to start your tree growing fruit."

There had been rumours all the week that "Sandy Claws" would bring his wife this year. There had been whispers even of a baby. So we could explain the second man; for the Eskimo men and women all dress alike in Labrador, which would account for "Mrs. Claws's" strange taste in clothes. A discreet silence was observed about her frozen whiskers.

A few minutes later, another large box was carried over to the room. It was full of emptiness, for the toys were on the tree long ago. But two strange masked and bewigged figures stumbled over the snow with it, to carry the little drama to its close. So complete was the faith in the unearthly origin of these our guests, that when the curtain went up, more than one voice was heard to be calling out for "Ma" and "Dad," while a lad of several summers was found hidden under the seat when it came his turn to go up and get his "prize."

And so Santa Claus came to St. Anthony, and brought a gift for us as well as presents for the children. Indeed, the best was the one he had kept for us, who had so unworthily thought that the outlook for a happy Christmas was but a poor one. Sleeping overhead in a clean white cot, free of pain and with a good fighting chance for his life, lay our bright-faced lad—Clem. The gift to us this Christmas Day was the chance to save his life. We would not have exchanged it for any gift we had ever heard of. At the old home, where doctors are plentiful, such a gift would be impossible.

The great, life-giving gift to the world that Christmas stands for was to be ours to thus faintly re-echo on this needy, far-off shore.

Christmas Eve in a Small Town
Norman Creighton

I would like to tell you how one town in the Maritimes is going to celebrate Christmas Eve. This is my own hometown of Hantsport, NS, which, as the name implies, is a port and a very busy one. It is only a small place, with about two thousand people, but we all have work to do. We have a certain amount of money to spend, and at this season of the year, we like to spend it.

Of course, our opportunities for spending money are not spectacular. There are no drinking places, none of those cocktail lounges or dimly lit bars where you peer in at the vague outlines of lonely folk nursing martinis. The nearest thing we have to a cocktail lounge is the restaurant on Main Street, where you can have coffee at the table beside the window and look out at the people passing by. They can look right back in and see you, and nod if they happen to know you, which they generally do.

We have no nightclubs, either, with entertainers and that kind of thing. But we do have singing. On Christmas Eve, the young people will be singing carols under the windows of shut-ins, while women will be delivering the baskets they have been busy packing to those who, because of age or illness, cannot get out.

The liveliest singing of all will be in the humming wires and clicking relays of the telephone building opposite the garage.

Messages will be coming through, from a niece in Vancouver and cousins in Sault Ste. Marie. The singing on those frosty wires makes a very happy chorus on Christmas Eve.

I wish you could see our decorations. Not that yours aren't lovely too, but ours are a little bit different. You see, Hantsport is a loading point for the fleet of gypsum boats that shuttle back and forth between here and New York. Sometimes they go to Baltimore, or Jacksonville, New Orleans, and Kingston, Jamaica. Some of the crewmembers live right here in town—or rather, their families live here. They have made sure those outside decorations can be seen from away down the bay, because on Christmas Eve, the men will be out on deck watching for the illuminated trees on the front lawns and the electric stars up on the roofs, as they steam in past Cape Blomidon and on to the fairway buoy.

At the dock to greet the boat will be rows of cars, their headlights flashing out a welcome from the wives and sweethearts of crewmembers from out of town. They may have driven up from Halifax, from Liverpool, and even from Yarmouth, 150 miles away, just to be here when the boat comes in.

She will be in port for only two hours, while ten thousand tons of gypsum pour into her hold. Then she blows three times, and the car horns on the dock answer, wishing her a good trip. At the final blast, the hawsers are thrown free, and she's off again to Baltimore.

What the men look forward to is the "trip off" every two months. It means a five- or six-day shore leave, to get acquainted with the baby and meet the neighbours.

Of course, Christmas Day is celebrated aboard ship. It is a holiday. The men just stand their watch, but there is no work to do out on deck. Then, at two o'clock, they sit down to a bang-up dinner—turkey, roast duck, baked ham, anything you want. Unlike the old windjammer days of salt herring and plum duff, these boys have a choice of roast beef and ice cream, Florida oranges and hearts of celery. But none of them would choose to be on the ship on Christmas Day if there was any way of getting ashore short of "paying off"—quitting the job.

I hope some of them have this trip off, so they can spend the holiday week at home and take part in those crucial last-minute decisions. Will we have the ham hot or cold? Does the silver need cleaning? Should we stuff the turkey tonight or leave it until tomorrow morning? Are you supposed to put onions in the dressing, or is that only for stuffed goose?

If the boat comes in before eleven thirty at night, the sailors will be able to attend the midnight service at St. Andrew's Anglican Church and join in the singing of "While Shepherds Watch Their Flock By Night," and then, at midnight, "Christians, Awake, Salute the Happy Morn."

I talked once with a man who could recall when Christmas morning was truly a miracle. His memory went back to the turn of the century, to a time when a strong man might earn a dollar and twenty cents a day cutting firewood—if he could cut a cord and a half. There were few Christmas presents then, but the expectation of that night was so great—the feeling that something miraculous was about to happen—that some of them would tiptoe out to the barn to see if it was indeed true that the cattle were kneeling in their stalls.

All that is gone now. We no longer believe such tales. And yet, as we listen to the bells chiming at midnight, we still antici-pate that something wonderful is waiting for us, to be revealed on Christmas morning. What will it be? It can come in such a simple package: a pair of hand-knit socks, some homemade rasp-berry preserves, or a loaf of strudel bread, frosted in red and green, baked by a friend who learned from her grandmother in Lunenburg how strudel bread is made.

So that is our Christmas Eve. It may not be quite as excit-ing as in Halifax or Saint John or Charlottetown, but the same expectations are here. We'll all have our lights on over the front door, waiting for someone to come.

So let's bring out a bottle of our homemade blackberry wine, that we may propose a toast. May *your* miracle come true—and may your Christmas be a happy one.

From *Ghosts Have Warm Hands*
Will R. Bird

There were clouds in the sky, and it was getting on for Christmas, so Mel and I started back to our units. We said a fond goodbye and vowed each other we would write—but never did. There was no 42nd at Mons. I had quite a search, but eventually located them on December 20 in a fine little village called Genval, on the outskirts of Brussels. It was evening, and as I went up the little street, I met Tommy. He stopped and shook his head. "At long last," he said. "You are really for it."

He told me that men who were three days over leave were getting a week in the clink. I was twenty-four days overdue. Furthermore, there were Pats at the end of the village and every billet was jammed to capacity, including the clink. Probably I would be sent to the city jail. What on earth had I been doing? I told him I had been on a tour of the south of France, the old battlefields, then Belgium. Oh yeah, and what had I used for money? A chap by name of Melvin Kidd. He had had two hundred dollars. Tommy shrugged. "I saw Arthur go into the orderly room," he said. "You had better get it over with."

Then I met Brown, and he was really worried about me. He had been in the old platoon with me at Aldershot, Nova Scotia, and right through. Whatever had possessed me? I would be stripped and probably given a month in the clink. "Thank you for being a Job's comforter," I said. "Where is the orderly room?"

He pointed to a lighted window in a building farther up the street. Across from it was a beautiful home with an ornamental iron fence and a gate with a swan on top. Huge bay windows extended upward to the second floor. There was a small balcony over the front door, and the walls were newly painted stucco. It was a house one would look at a second time. "Some joint," I remarked.

"You needn't look at it," said Brown. "The colonel tried to locate there and the lady turned him down cold. His batman told us. It's the home of the head electrician of Brussels."

I swung along and went into the orderly room, put my pack and rifle in a corner. Major Arthur was talking with the company sergeant-major, and the orderly sergeant was at a desk. They stopped speaking and stared. I saluted. "Well," said the major. "You did come back. We thought you had gone to Canada."

"It's likely I would have if there had been a chance, sir," I said.

The major moved to a corner, where he stood and talked in a low tone with the sergeant-major. Presently he turned, waved a hand at me, and went out. "Let's get it over with," I said to the sergeant-major. "Where's the clink?"

"You," he said, shaking his head, "are the luckiest guy in the Forty-Second. Arthur never knew how they had held up your leave. I've heard rumours he gave them a talk they won't forget. The orders are on the desk. You will carry on as from now. You will be our orderly sergeant. But don't start celebrating. There is no accommodation anywhere. You will have to make the best of it on this floor."

He put on his balmoral and walked out. The sergeant followed him, and I could see vast disappointment on his leathery visage. I sat and looked at the usual routine orders. There was nothing difficult. Being orderly sergeant was really a cinch. It kept one off parade, and wise to all that was going on. The fire had died in the stove, and a glance told me all the rationed fuel for the day had been used. I sat a moment before making my decision. Leaving the light on and the door unlocked, I took my pack and rifle, walked across the road, in through the swan gate, and pressed the bell button beside the elaborate front door.

The woman who appeared was a beautiful lady. She had perfect poise and spoke excellent English. I told her my circumstances carefully, explained I had heard she refused lodging to our colonel, and added that only the idea of a night on the orderly room floor gave me courage to ring her bell. She listened courteously. Her eyes twinkled, and she nodded. "You are an interesting talker," she said. "I think we will get on well. Turn out your light and lock up and come back. Leave your pack here."

It was hard to believe. When I found myself in a beautiful bed in one of the front bedrooms, with magnificent furniture and deep rugs on the floor, I had to sit up and gloat over my surroundings. I had not had such accommodation before in my life. Everything spoke of wealth and culture and comfort.

In the morning I tried to go down without making any noise, but Madame was awaiting me, smiling. "I know you must be at your office," she said, "and do not think you would like breakfast in our dining room. So I have it for you in the kitchen."

There was toast and tea, eggs and bacon, and Madame in a soft negligee on the other side of the table. "Please don't think this is entirely pity on you for your predicament," she said. "Partly, it is a bit of selfishness on my side of the situation. My husband is very busy with so many troops in barracks and so many Christmas entertainments in the offing. There is enormous demand for electricity. He comes in late and goes out early. Everyone is busy at this season, and I like company. So if you do not mind, we will have much conversation and I will learn about Canada. Now I want you to meet Carmen, our only child."

Carmen was ten and gave every promise of being as beautiful as her mother. She had only a word or two of English and was quite shy, but managed to ask if she might visit me in the orderly room after school. I told her she was welcome at any time.

Our ration of fuel arrived as I opened the orderly room and soon I had a fire going. I performed the routine duties. Then mail arrived, and there were four parcels for me. There were also written instructions that, since the battalion might move at any time, the parcels for those recently gone on leave were to be opened, and only personal gifts such as razors or a watch or flashlight were to be carried. All candy and cakes were to be discarded.

After school was out, in came Carmen with two companions her own age, shy little girls who stood in the background. Carmen came over and deliberately climbed on my knee, put her arms around my neck and gave me a warm kiss. Her action had me almost flabbergasted, but I tried to act perfectly natural, opened a drawer of the desk, and handed her three candy bars. There was no such candy in Belgium, and her face fairly shone. She had a small battle with herself, then slid down, crossed the floor, and presented each watching girl with a bar. Then the three of them were munching with little squeals of pleasure. Each day the procedure was the same, though there were occasionally different playmates. And Carmen was very smart in picking up English, much smarter than I in learning her French.

Now there were Christmas decorations going up everywhere. Madame introduced me to her husband, a fine-looking man with a black moustache, who promptly told me I must have Christmas dinner with them. It would be at noon and they could not take "no" for an answer.

All our men were in extremely high spirits, except Farmer. There were crude characters staying a day or so over the ten allotted them for 1918, and he was hard-pressed to find room for them all in the clink. The officers, however, were more human, and there was no drill or parade to bother anyone. Half the lads in trouble over leave were released. Perhaps someone had nerve enough to remind company commanders that the officers had had three times as much leave as the men, and had seen one-third as much action.

The Christmas dinner was a grand affair. There were six guests, one the brother of the host, a younger man with a fine tenor voice who spoke good English and was the life of the party. There was plenty of champagne and plenty of toasts—the first being to Canada, to which I was obliged to respond. Not having had any acquaintance with champagne, I was afraid of it, but Madame assured me it was of the finest quality and would not have much effect if I did not take too much. So I sipped eleven to twelve toasts, then the others got something stronger with the dessert. It was enough to get the brother in good voice, and he sang two or three songs. Finally everyone was laughing and shouting, and he jumped up to the table, getting a footing among the silver and china, and commenced a gay song having to do with a penurious bridegroom bargaining with an innkeeper for a room at the beginning of his honeymoon. It would never be sung in English at any dinner in my hometown, but everyone laughed uproariously, and at points he called to me in English explanations of each verse.

The dinner ended at three, and our regimental Christmas dinner began at five. Many Belgian dignitaries and their wives were present in finest bib and tucker, and the liquid refreshments flowed generously. By seven, I was on the dance floor with awkward feet, unable to release myself from a stout, determined Belgian lady with a slight moustache, who had received scant attention from the lieutenant who was her dinner companion. She was half-drunk and quite determined to make a night of it. Fortunately for me, a garter or something gave way and she had to retire to make repairs. In that moment, I was among the missing, and had a good, long walk in fresh air to help the digestion after two dinners, and to have a chance to think of Christmas in the Canadian town I called home.

The Old School Concerts
Bud Ings

S anta Claus had just finished passing out his Christmas concert presents to all the children, saving the teacher's for the last. I thought she was lucky: Santa gave her a big hug and tried to kiss her. I could see that his big beard was in the way. She gently pushed him to the side of the stage, and he made a flying leap for the door, shouting, "Merry Christmas, everyone!" and in a few seconds disappeared into the night.

The year was 1932. I was only six years old, and I just had to see the reindeer waiting outside for their driver. Some men were blocking my way, standing at the back of the school next to the entrance. When they realized that I was trying desperately to get out to see Santa's team, they lifted me up and out to the door. "Get him out fast or the reindeer will be gone!" one of them shouted.

I ran toward the road, only to hear the tinkling of bells in the distance. I had just missed seeing Santa with his red sleigh. But I could hear the bells in the distance, and I knew they had to be Santa's.

That event alone would have made the Christmas concerts at our school memorable for me. But in all my years in that one-room school in Mount Herbert, the concerts were the highlight of the festive season—as they were in schools across the Island.

In the late fall, the teacher began preparing the program, with short skits, recitations, monologues, and musical numbers.

In our school, the concerts always featured a fiddler and someone playing an old organ borrowed from the church.

Our teacher made sure that her concert date appeared in the "coming events" section of the newspaper very early in December. To have another concert in the next district on the same night would have been a disaster.

Cutting down the Christmas tree in the woods was a task the big boys loved. If the tree they brought back wasn't suitable, the teacher ordered them back to the woods for a better one. We thought this was a slick way to miss concert practices and horse around in the woods, but the teacher wasn't fooled: she kept us after school to learn our parts. The girls, considered to be more careful than the boys about handling delicate ornaments, had the honour of decorating the tree and making it look magical. On the night of the concert, candles were lighted and attached to the branches with tin clamps. A bucket of water was kept close by in case of fire.

A special part of the evening came when all the students sang Christmas choruses, standing on the wobbly old stage that had been erected for the occasion. When the gang hit on a familiar song like "Jingle Bells," the entire audience joined in, clapping hands.

The concerts were definitely a community affair. The Women's Institute helped the teacher make costumes for the skits, and a "fudge committee" saw that there was a plentiful supply of candy on the big night. It was passed around for everyone to enjoy. A schoolroom built for about thirty students was packed with about seventy-five people, sitting and standing shoulder to shoulder. The old pot-bellied stove in the centre of the room gave off waves of heat, forcing almost everyone to take off coats and sweaters.

Even Santa Claus was part of the community effort. In fact, he was quite at home in our district—a fact of which I was blissfully unaware the night of my first school concert. All I knew that night was that I had heard his sleigh bells, and that the sound was magical; and for years afterwards, nobody could convince me otherwise.

A Gift to Last
Alistair Cameron

I remember Christmas in years that are long since past, but the memory of Christmas 1929 encircles me with a warmth and wonder that draws me back down through the years at Christmastime.

This was our first Christmas in Canada. The excitement of the Christmas concert, the glittering Christmas tree, and the cheery well-wishes of the Kirkland people raised the commonplace to a scene of song, laughter, and mirth. Now it was over. Back in the farm kitchen of the McDougall place, we sat, chatted, and drank tea, recalling the dialogues, readings, tableaus, and songs. The teacher, Miss Annie Graham, had put a lot of work into the preparation of the concert, and it was no surprise when it went over without a hitch. My dad, who had consented to a request to "Give us a tune on your accordion," did himself proud as he played a fast-paced medley of Scottish tunes that caused toes to tap and the floorboards of the old Orange Hall in Kirkland to creak in protest. The fragrance of pine, the tang of frosted air, the smiling eyes and breathless expectancy, were all part of an evening echoing the thought that Christmas was in the air.

Our Scottish Christmases were somewhat subdued. In that part of the Highlands where we lived before coming to Canada, Christmas was regarded as a holy day. Psalms were sung in preference to carols. Of course Santa Claus came, and he left one present for each child and that was all, for our Santa was a thrifty wee man. Now, as we sat in the warmth of the farmhouse kitchen, we thought of those friends and relatives far across the sea. We would not be going home for Christmas, except in memory.

How quiet the house was this night. The snap of tamarack in the kitchen stove was the only sound, except for an occasional sigh coming from the direction of Mother's chair in the corner. My own thoughts that night were with a snuggly pup that used to chase me through the heather. How I hated to give him up. Poor wee dog, he hated to give me up too.

Christmas fell on a Wednesday that year. A brisk and biting breeze followed us between house and barn as we did the chores. The smoke curling upward from the chimney signalled a welcome warmth around the kitchen stove.

Although we did not go in for a big Christmas feast in Scotland (that was something that was part of bringing in the New Year, with its traditional first footing and "Auld Lang Syne"), Mother decided because this was our first Christmas in Canada, and because it was a custom here, a special meal would be prepared; but nothing elaborate, mind you. Nothing must take away from the real meaning of Christmas—the birth of the Christ child in a stable long ago. It would be a meal of thanksgiving, she said. And so the plumpest hen in the henhouse lost her head that day. No fancy spiced cakes, no mouth-watering mincemeat pies, no extras, nothing fancy, just plain grub: fowl, potatoes, vegetables, bread and butter, and good, strong tea would be our supper on that Christmas night in 1929.

By mid-afternoon, the wind had died down. A stillness fell over the countryside. In the barn close by, Bessie, one of the cows, let out an exuberant moo. No doubt it was her way of thanking Dad for the extra portion of chopped turnips that all of the cows enjoyed that day. My sentimental dad was remembering that both man and beast shared in the glory and wonder of that first Christmas. So each beast in his care relished an extra ration of oats or turnips, which quickly disappeared with much huffing and munching.

It was warm and cozy in the byre. The heat generated by the animals felt good to one coming in from the lowering temperature outside. It was time to let the cows out for their daily exercise around the barnyard, and a thirst-quenching drink from the sturdy hogshead that was kept continually filled by one of the many springs on the farm. In due time the animals were back in their stalls, wallowing contentedly in their beds of clean, fresh straw. The chores were finished for the night and barn doors tightly barred. It was suppertime. The thought of roast hen had been uppermost in my mind all afternoon. I had been promised a drumstick and I longed now to taste it, along with the mashed potatoes and brown gravy that went with it.

Like a small army, my dad, and my brothers Geordie and Bill, with me in the rear, wended our way from the barn to the house, conscious of the nip of frost on our ears. It was then that we saw "him."

Trudging down the temporary sled road through the McDougalls' field came a man. His head was bent, occasionally lifted to scan the sky overhead. A long overcoat nearly hid the leather-topped gum rubbers into which he had tucked the bottoms of his blue coveralls. He was carrying a black case. "It can't be the Watkins man," said Geordie. "He was here yesterday." As he came nearer, we saw that the case he was carrying was one to hold a violin.

Inside the house, we removed our outside togs and waited for the knock on the kitchen door. It never came. Instead, the door opened, and on the threshold stood the stranger. "Come away in," my mother said. "You are just in time for supper." Hospitality was second nature to her, and besides, she would be the first to remind you of the words in the Good Book, "I was a stranger and ye took me in."

After brushing the snow from his boots, our guest stuck out his hand, cold, and calloused from hard work. "My name is Basil McIntyre. I've come to wish you a merry Christmas." We all shook hands in turn. We liked this man with the firm grip and the friendly, open face.

Later, sitting around the table, Basil told us many interesting things about Kirkland and its people. We learned of the close family relationships. The names Graham, Taylor, Bustard, Kennedy, and Dickison were all prominent in the community. Hard working and deeply honourable, as were the Jacksons, Kidneys, Andersons, Griffins, and Nicholsons. In no time, we felt that we knew our neighbours much better. The lonely feeling that had enfolded us earlier in the day gradually faded away. It was a grand Christmas.

In the parlour, my brother Bill had kindled a fire in the box-like stove with the isinglass windows in its door, through which the fire cast a cheery glow. The parlour was a special place not used much, but tonight was special. We had a guest.

Conversation came to a stop when Basil brought out his violin. I can see him now as he applied rosin to the bow, turning the pegs to get the right pitch and then plucking the strings to bring out "Pop Goes The Weasel." Soon old country airs filled the room. Irish reels and jigs made the blood run faster. In a softer mood came "Juanita," "Moonlight on the Colorado," "Red Wing," and many more. When the clock struck ten, Mother went to the kitchen to put the kettle on. With the help of my sister, Molly, a tasty lunch was passed around. We were not hungry. The stuffed satisfaction of the Christmas hen stayed with us still. A good cup of tea, though, is never amiss, and we enjoyed this one particularly.

There was a time of quietness, each of us with our own thoughts. I looked at Basil sitting on the red plush platform rocker with violin in one hand, bow in the other, a faraway look in his eyes as he gazed at the reflected light of the fire through the isinglass in the stove door.

Slowly he raised the violin to his chin, gently he stroked the strings, and music, soft and sweet, stirred our hearts. In the enjoyment of listening to the jigs and reels, we had overlooked the sometimes harsh and squeaky sounds, but this was different. With eyes closed now, he continued to play, the notes softly fading away to a whisper. The room seemed quieter than before. Even the cat on the rug in front of the fire had stopped his purring.

Mother was the first to speak when the tune had ended. "My, that was beautiful," she said. "What is it called?"

Basil looked stunned. "You mean you don't know it?"

"No," Mother said. "We've never heard it before. It's a bonny tune. Please play it again."

As Basil played, Mother and I hummed the melody. Only when the notes had wafted away for the second time did Basil tell us the name of the piece that had such a heartfelt effect on all of us. "It's an old hymn," he said. "It's called 'Silent Night.' It's a wonder you haven't heard it. Some folks call it a carol."

"Our kirk did not go in much for carols," Mother explained. "We always sang the old Presbyterian hymns and psalms. I do remember that we used to sing 'Once in Royal David's City' at Christmas, but never 'Silent Night.'"

I remember going over to the old pump organ that stood against the west wall, seeing the red plush sofa that was too good to sit on, picking up an old hymn book with its brownish-yellow cover with a descending angel on it and the title *The Voice of Melody* boldly displayed; and in it I found what I was looking for, and read aloud:

> *Silent night, holy night,*
> *All is calm, all is bright,*
> *Round yon Virgin Mother and Child,*
> *Holy infant so tender and mild,*
> *Sleep in heavenly peace,*
> *Sleep in heavenly peace.*

When I came to the words in the last verse:

Wondrous star, lend thy light,
Let us with the angels sing,
Al-le-lu-ia to our King,
Christ the Saviour is born,

a feeling of contentment, wonder, and thankfulness was all around us. That faraway stable somehow felt very close that night.

Basil declined my parents' invitation to stay all night. "I must be gettin' home," he said. "I can sleep better in my own bed."

We followed him out onto the veranda. Not a breath of wind flurried the snow that covered the fields around us. Never did the moon shine so bright. Never was a night as still as this. Mother turned down the lamps. The old wall clock struck twelve, Christmas 1929 was over.

Our first Christmas in Canada. What could have been a lonely and self-pitying time for us was turned into a strangely happy event, all because an old man with a scarred violin was guided to our door. I am sure that fate sent him there.

Of all the gifts that Christmas has brought through the years, Basil's gift to us that night is cherished more than any. A simple tune reminding us of a babe born under the floor of the world, warmed by the breath of animals in a stable. Silent night, holy night, surely a gift to last.

About the Contributors

Nova Scotian **WILL R. BIRD** served with the 42nd Battalion of the Canadian Expeditionary Forces in France and Belgium during World War One, and his experiences as a soldier deeply influenced his writing. He wrote stories, articles, and memoirs based on the diaries he kept throughout 1917 and 1918, relating in poignant personal terms what it meant to live through the agony of war. His many published books include *Here Stays Good Yorkshire*, *The North Shore Regiment*, and *Ghosts Have Warm Hands*.

ERNEST BUCKLER was born in Dalhousie West, Nova Scotia, in 1908. He studied at Dalhousie University, and then the University of Toronto, before returning to his home province in 1936. While living on his farm near Bridgetown, Buckler wrote a number of important works, including the fictional memoir *Ox Bells and Butterflies*, the Leacock Award–winning *Whirligig*, and his masterpiece, the novel *The Mountain and the Valley*.

Born in Scotland in 1917, author **ALISTAIR CAMERON** moved with his parents to the Upper St. John River Valley in 1929. He wrote several memoirs about his life and the immigrant experience, including *Milestones & Memories* and *Aberdeen It Was Not*.

A CBC radio broadcaster from the 1940s through the 1970s, **NORMAN CREIGHTON** was well known for his enjoyable and accurate accounts of traditional life in Nova Scotia. Many of his weekly talks from the 1960s and 1970s have been collected in the anthologies *Talk About the Maritimes* and *Talk About the Valley*.

Like his father, John Curtis, author **WAYNE CURTIS** was born in the rural community of Keenan, New Brunswick, which is near Blackville. Both were educated at local schoolhouses, but John attended only sporadically, and eventually quit to work for his father in the lumber woods. It is John's school memory that Wayne relates in "My Christmas Concert." Wayne has authored many books, the most recent of which is *Long Ago and Far Away: A Miramichi Family Memoir*. You can find him online at www.waynecurtis.ca.

DAVID GOSS is a celebrated and prolific New Brunswick storyteller. His books include *Saint John Curiosities*, *It Happened in New Brunswick*, *Tall Tales & Curious Happenings*, and the brand-new *Only in New Brunswick*. He lives in West Saint John, where he runs "Walks n' Talks," a community tour business that introduces residents and visitors to local history.

SIR WILFRED T. GRENFELL was a missionary, a medical doctor, and an author. He focused much of his writing on his experiences as a doctor in northern Newfoundland and Labrador, and published several books, including *Adrift on an Ice-Pan*, *Vikings of To-day*, and his autobiography, *A Labrador Doctor*.

At age twenty-six, Dartmouth native **JOHN HUGHES** became a Canadian hero when he entered the gruelling BOC Challenge—an around-the-world, solo yacht race that demands the best of the world's most skilled sailors. Hughes became the youngest competitor and the first Canadian to enter and finish this punishing race. His memoir *The Sailing Spirit* recounts the dangers and triumphs he experienced as a contestant in the Challenge.

Prince Edward Island's answer to James Herriot, **BUD INGS** was born on the Island in 1926, and graduated from the Ontario Veterinary College in 1952. He practiced in rural PEI for many years, and in December 2009 he was inducted into the Atlantic Agricultural Hall of Fame. He has so far published two memoirs of his experiences as a rural veterinarian: *Mud, Sweat and Tears* and *Vet Behind the Years*.

BOB KROLL has written for the broadcast industry for more than thirty-five years, including CBC radio dramas, television documentaries, and historical docu-dramas for Canadian and American museums. He is the author of the novel *Intimate Fragments* and the brand-new *Rogues and Rascals: True Stories of Maritime Lives and Legends*.

GEORGE LITTLE is a former English teacher at Simonds High School in Saint John, and was head of the New Brunswick New Democratic Party for eight years. He is the author of the short-story collection *The Many Deaths of George Robertson*.

Cape Breton–born humourist **ANDY MACDONALD** has authored five collections of memoirs, including *Bread and Molasses, Don't Slip on the Soap*, and *'Tis Me Again, B'y!* Each relates tales of his boyhood and adult years, told with his signature brand of Maritime wit.

Born and raised on Prince Edward Island, **LUCY MAUD MONTGOMERY** is the esteemed author of *Anne of Green Gables*, *Emily of New Moon*, *Chronicles of Avonlea*, and numerous other novels, short stories, poems, and journals. She is perhaps Atlantic Canada's best-loved author.

About the Contributors

One of Canada's most enduring writers, **ALDEN NOWLAN** has left a legacy of stories that never fail to surprise and delight readers. His impressive bibliography of fiction, plays, poetry, and essays includes *Will Ye Let the Mummers In?*, *Double Exposure*, and the collection *Bread, Wine and Salt*, which won the 1967 Governor General's Award for poetry.

MICHAEL O. NOWLAN was born in Chatham, New Brunswick. He spent thirty-five years as a schoolteacher, most of them in Oromocto, where he has lived since 1964. He has edited or written more than twenty books, including the poetry collection *The Other Side* and the Christmas anthology *The Last Bell*. He is also an avid stamp collector, and has written many medal-winning articles on the subject. He was very honoured when he was admitted to the honourary degree of Doctor of Letters by St. Thomas University in 2010.

BRUCE NUNN—a storyteller who became known as Mr. Nova Scotia Know-It-All on CBC Radio—is the author of six Atlantic Canadian books, including *Buddy the Bluenose Reindeer*, *Buddy the Bluenose Reindeer and the Boston Christmas Tree Adventure*, and his latest, *Nova Scotia's Curious Connections*. He was born in Antigonish, Nova Scotia.

New Brunswick–born **DAVID ADAMS RICHARDS** is an accomplished writer of fiction, nonfiction, poetry, and screenplays, and one of the only writers to win the Governor General's Award for both fiction and nonfiction. His instantly recognizable and deeply memorable writing style has made him one of Canada's best known and most highly acclaimed authors. His works include *Nights Below Station Street* (the first book in his Miramichi trilogy), *Mercy Among the Children*, and his latest novel, *Incidents in the Life of Markus Paul*.

Born and raised in Newfoundland, and a longtime resident of Nova Scotia, artist and naturalist **GARY L. SAUNDERS** is known for infusing his passion for the Atlantic provinces into his writing. He has published a range of nonfiction titles, including *Trees of Nova Scotia, Discover Nova Scotia: The Ultimate Nature Guide*, and the childhood memoir *Free Wind Home*.

JENNIFER (Prosser) WADE was born in India, although she comes from an old Yarmouth County, Nova Scotia, family. She is an internationally renowned human rights worker and justice advocate, as well as a writer and teacher. After doing post-graduate work in London, England, she worked with the Civil Rights Movement in Georgia, where she also taught writing at Emory University. She holds a BA and an honourary Doctor of Letters degree from the University of New Brunswick. Presently she lives in Vancouver, BC.

DOROTHY WINSLOW WRIGHT is an internationally published author and poet whose work has appeared in numerous literary anthologies and magazines, including the *Atlantic Advocate*, where "Angel Wings" was first published. These days, she makes her home in Honolulu, Hawaii.

Sources

Bird, Will R. *Ghosts Have Warm Hands*. (Toronto: Clarke, Irwin & Company, 1968), 235–239.

Buckler, Ernest. "Return Trip To Christmas." *Thanks for Listening*. Ed. Marta Dvorak. (Waterloo: Wilfrid Laurier University Press, 2004), 126–142.

Cameron, Alistair. "A Gift to Last." *Aberdeen It Was Not*. (Hartland: Hartland Publishing, 1982), 55–59.

Creighton, Norman. "Christmas Eve in a Small Town." *Talk About the Maritimes*. Ed. Hilary Sircom. (Halifax: Nimbus Publishing, 1998), 151–153.

Curtis, Wayne. "My Christmas Concert." *Telegraph-Journal* (Dec. 2010).

Goss, David. "New Brunswick's First Santa Claus." *Tall Tales & Curious Happenings* (Halifax: Nimbus Publishing, 2002), 214–217.

Grenfell, Wilfred T. "How Santa Claus Came to Cape St. Anthony." *Christmas In Newfoundland and Labrador*. Ed. D. W. S. Ryan. (St. John's: Jesperson Press, 1988), 36–42.

Hughes, John. *The Sailing Spirit*. (Toronto: McLelland-Bantam, 1988), 88–92.

Ings, Bud. "The Old Schools Concerts." *Vet Behind the Years* (Charlottetown: Acorn Press, 2010), 15–17.

Kroll, Bob. "Lucky Stars." *Chronicle Herald* (24 Dec. 1993): B1.

Little, George. "Christmas Mittens." *Atlantic Advocate* (Dec. 1989), 21–23.

MacDonald, Andy. *Bread and Molasses.* (Don Mills: Musson Book Company, 1986), 59–60.

Montgomery, Lucy Maud. "A Christmas Mistake." *The Fitzhenry & Whiteside Fireside Book of Canadian Christmas.* Ed. Patrick Crean. (Markham: Fitzhenry & Whiteside Publishing, 1986), 34–40.

Nowlan, Alden. "Will Ye Let the Mummers In?" *Will Ye Let the Mummers In?* (Toronto: Irwin Publishing, 1984), 60–75.

Nowlan, Michael O. "The Last Bell." *Atlantic Advocate* (Dec. 1977), 20–23.

Richards, David Adams. "The Child and the Boy." *Atlantic Advocate* (Dec. 1971), 23+.

Saunders, Gary L. "The Winter House." *September Christmas.* (St. John's: Breakwater Books, 1992), 41–49.

Wade, Jennifer. "The Celluloid Angel." *Atlantic Advocate* (Dec. 1989), 32–33.

Sources

Wright, Dorothy Winslow. "Angel Wings." *Atlantic Advocate* (Dec. 1990), 42–43.